T0316502

Glass Ceilings: Women in South African Media Houses
© Copyright 2018 Gender Links.
ISBN: 978-0-620-81704-2

Gender Links
9 Derrick Avenue
Cyrildene, 2198
Johannesburg, South Africa
Phone: 27 11 029 0006/ 27 11 028 2410
Email: media@genderlinks.org.za

Website: www.genderlinks.org.za
Sanef: www.sanef.org.za/

Authors: Glenda Daniels, Tarisai Nyamweda,
Collin Nxumalo and Barbara Ludman
Editor: Colleen Lowe Morna

Cover photo: Petronella Ngonyama, an aspiring
journalist shoots a video of the Gender and Media
Diversity Centre Community of Practice.
Photo: Zoto Razanadratefa.

Back cover photo: Mamma Kgamane from Zebediela
FM speaking at a media gender policies workshop in
Polokwane. Photo: Tarisai Nyamweda

Design and Layout: Debi Lee Designs
Printer: Scratch Solutions
Sponsors: Media Development and Diversity Agency
(MDDA)

This report has been produced with the full financial
assistance of the Media Development and Diversity
Agency (MDDA). The views expressed herein are those
of Gender Links (GL) and the South African National
Editors Forum (Sanef) and can therefore in no way
be taken to reflect the official opinion of the MDDA.

Acknowledgements

The Glass Ceilings research, which builds on an initial study undertaken by Gender Links (GL) and the South African National Editors Forum (Sanef) in 2007 and the broader Southern African Glass Ceiling project of 2009, provides progress on gender in South African newsrooms.

GL and Sanef designed, coordinated and managed the research with support from the Media Development and Diversity Agency (MDDA). The research team comprised a mix of students and academics: Patricia Handley, Maud Blose, Madikana Matjila, Mauwane Raophala, Sindiso Ndlovu, Sakhile Dube, Bongane Gasela, Robyn Evans, Petronella Ngonyama and Helen Grange. Collin Nxumalo conducted the in-depth interviews with women journalists. Monica Bandeira analysed the data.

Professor Glenda Daniels (associate professor in Media Studies, University of the Witwatersrand and Chair of Sanef's Diversity and Ethics Committee); Tarisai Nyamweda (GL Media Manager) and Barbara Ludman (freelance editor) wrote the report. Professor Ylva Rodny-Gumede and Dr Kate Skinner peer reviewed the report. GL CEO Colleen Lowe Morna edited the report.

Acronyms

ABC	Australian Broadcasting Corporation
AIP	Association of Independent Publishers
ANC	African National Congress
BCCSA	Broadcasting Complaints Commission of South Africa
BDPA	Beijing Declaration and Platform for Action
CNN	Cable News Network
CPJ	Committee to Protect Journalists
FXI	Freedom of Expression Institute
GAMAG	Global Alliance on Media and Gender
GL	Gender Links
ICT	Information and Communications Technology
IWMF	International Women's Media Foundation
JSE	Johannesburg Stock Exchange
MAT	Media Appeals Tribunal
MDDA	Media Development and Diversity Agency
MWASA	Media Workers Association of South Africa
PDMTTT	Print and Digital Media Transformation Task Team
SA	South Africa
SABC	South African Broadcasting Corporation
SADC	Southern African Development Community
Sanef	South African National Editors Forum
SAUJ	South African Union of Journalists
UN	United Nations
UNESCO	United Nations Educational, Scientific and Cultural Organization
UNISA	University of South Africa

Contents

Foreword

By Mahlatse Mahlase (nee Gallens), Chair, Sanef

The following random quote celebrating women's tenacity has stayed with me: "Here's to strong women. May we know them. May we be them. May we raise them."

When I was asked about the defining moments in my career as a woman journalist, the many crises that have been my journey in journalism came flooding in. How does one pick one or a few from the many defining moments the rich world of journalism has to offer?

Should it be the sexism, not only in the workplace but also from newsmakers, especially as a political reporter? The politicians who hit on me first before I even requested an interview or when I arrived for the interview and who felt it was okay to say something about the size of my bum or comment on my legs...

Recently one man told me to come wearing a dress, and despite the current freezing temperature in Joburg, he said, "Don't wear stockings". South African journalists will recall that during the president's first term, certain staff in his office actually asked management of the public broadcaster to "please not have any women in the presidential press corps", and I recall they argued that they wanted to avoid "potential" scandals. But the broadcaster complied.

Or should it be about the ageism in our industry? "She is still too young to be a boss," I was once told to my face. Never mind that I had been acting in the position for months, managing men who define your ability to lead, with their starting premise being that you are a woman.

Or, of course, if you are generally loud like I am (or passionate, as I choose to define it) and you are told halfway through making your point, "don't be emotional". There are of course the women who openly say male bosses are just better - never mind that the one before hardly bothered to pitch for work and if he did his office smelled like a cheap bar.

Or should it be about the racism still in parts of our industry - not only in terms of who is leading the newsroom or owns the media houses but who is chosen as thought leaders in our society?

When I started at the South African Broadcasting Corporation (SABC) at the tender age of 18, I was asked if they should use my voice or get someone to do a voice-over for my script. It went over my head then that because I am black, my accent might not be right for the precious SAfm listeners of the English news on SABC3.

There was also the waking up in sweat and panic, asking yourself if you should have gone on that dinner date instead of covering the earthquake in Haiti, or relocated to the Democratic Republic of Congo, ending a relationship. And now that

I have a relationship, I am battling to find a balance between work and life, and I realise that being a wife, mother and journalist requires you to have some supernatural powers.

Was the defining moment during the last three years of working for the public broadcaster led by a narcissist (and I am not exaggerating - he spoke of himself in the third person, declared himself the alpha and omega and openly threatened that it was his way or the highway)? His way of course was all about destroying the tenets of our founding Constitution that had declared the public broadcaster the pivot of our democracy. Towards the 2014 elections, he wanted to silence the opposition, demanded we report a skewed reality of my beloved country... We were on opposite sides.

All these are not the defining moments in my career. They are unfortunately the reality that is our life, whether in Africa or the so-called Western world. The difference might be degrees.

My defining moment came when I was preparing this piece. For all these hurdles I had to jump over there was a woman who held my hand, shone the light in what was a dark tunnel, challenged me to take the next step when I doubted my own abilities. The woman who is always willing to read through my piece when I doubt my own thoughts, or the one who calls me out on the nonsense I am writing and the one who risked her own job when the narcissist wanted to fire me for daring to challenge him. They have always been my pillars of strength through the hard times, the wings I needed as I tried to move up my career and the pearls of wisdom when life happened.

The industry is slowly changing; more women are entering senior roles but we would be naive to think sexism, racism and male chauvinism will end in our lifetime

The 2018 Glass Ceiling research finds that the proportion of women senior managers has increased from 35% in 2009 to 46% in 2018 and in top management from 25% in 2009 to 36% in 2018. But the proportion of women on boards has declined. The proportion of black women in top management has increased from 6% in 2006 to 30% at present but this is still far from black men at 50%.

In the three media houses that provided wage data, women earn on average 23% less than men, compared to 17% in 2009. The new reality in newsrooms is a few senior men at the top, and a battalion of junior staff running the social media platforms that are fast replacing the more traditional forms of media. With social media has come a new threat felt acutely by women in the media - the cyber misogyny highlighted for the first time in the study.

There are young journalists afraid to speak out because they fear losing their jobs. We dedicate this third edition of the *Glass Ceilings in South African Media* to them, and to all the strong women before them, on whose shoulders we stand. We urge them, in this age of the #MeToo and #TotalShutdown movements, to claim the spaces that threaten to silence them: to speak up, and speak out.

"Here's to strong women. May we know them. May we be them. May we raise them."

(Mahlatse Mahlase, chairperson of Sanef, is Eye Witness News (EWN) group editor in chief. This is an edited version of a speech she delivered at the Women in News Summit in Durban on 7 June 2017).

Executive Summary

On 1 August 2018 South African women, galvanised by the #TotalShutdown campaign, marched to the Union Buildings to declare that they had nothing to celebrate during Women's Month. President Cyril Ramaphosa agreed to convene a summit, now scheduled for 1-2 November.   *Photo: Thandokuhle Dlamini*

The challenges for women in the South African media are becoming less about numbers, and more about the underlying sexism in the media, with new threats like cyber misogyny emerging, according to the third *Glass Ceilings* survey[1] launched on 19 October 2018[2].

The study - undertaken by the South African National Editors Forum (Sanef) and Gender Links (GL) - finds that there have been dramatic shifts in the race and gender composition of media houses

since 2006. Black men now comprise half of top media managers. The proportion of black women in *top* media management has increased fivefold but is still 20 percentage points lower than black men. Black women, who comprise 46% of the population, constitute 40% of *senior* managers in the media, suggesting that change is on the way.

But it comes at a turbulent time. With new media forms sweeping across the landscape, South Africa fits into the global media pattern of traumatic job losses, random and messy digitisation processes, a huge downturn in advertising revenue and a decline in sales and circulation. While only three out of the 59 media houses that participated in the

---

[1] The other two studies were undertaken in 2006 and 2009. The 2009 study formed part of a SADC-wide study.
[1] On 19 October 1977, the apartheid government banned The World and Weekend World as well as Pro Veritate, a religious publication that was run by the late Beyers Naude. The day was later known as Black Wednesday. It is commemorated as South Africa's national media freedom day.

study gave data on wages, this and general perceptions suggest a growing *gender wage gap* as a result of fewer senior and top managers and a growing throng of junior cadets running the social media platforms of media houses.

A new threat against women has also emerged in the form of the *cyber misogyny* that includes some of the ugliest forms of sexism being used to try and silence media women. But the media is operating in a climate of the #MeToo movement globally and the #Totalshutdown movement nationally, which has seen an increased assertiveness from women about sexism and patriarchal domination.

Table I: Key indicators of Women in the South African Media 2018 vs 2009			
	Female 2018 %	Female 2009 %	Variance (2018 minus 2009) Percentage points
Percentage of employees by sex			
Overall	49	50	-1
Print	53		
Television	52		
Online	51		
Radio	48		
OCCUPATIONAL LEVELS			
Unskilled	60	23	37
Semi-skilled	74	55	19
Skilled technical	38	51	-13
Professionally qualified	52	42	10
Board of directors	19	38	-19
Senior management	46	35	11
Top management	36	25	11
DEPARTMENTS			
Finance and Administration	79	61	18
Advertising/Marketing	53	59	-6
Editorial	53	52	1
Production	42	66	-24
Design	32	34	-2
Distribution	30	33	-3
Technical	18	23	-5
CONDITIONS OF EMPLOYMENT			
Part time	56	61	-5
Full time, fixed term contract	50	55	-5
Full time open ended contract	53	49	4

The 2018 study, that took place between December 2017 and October 2018, aimed to assess progress ten years since the last Glass Ceilings Project, and also 25 years into democracy. Specific objectives included:

- To assess progress in achieving gender equality in the media, at decision-making and other levels.
- To assess progress in transforming work culture in the media from a gender perspective, and measure the gender gap in earnings in the media.

- To assess the gendered impact of the digital revolution on the composition, earnings and work culture in the media.
- To use the findings to develop strategic interventions to ensure gender equality in the media by 2030, in line with the Post-2015 SADC Protocol on Gender and Development.

The study took place in the context of the Southern African Development Community (SADC) Protocol on Gender and Development that calls for the mainstreaming of gender in all media laws, policies and training. It urges the media to achieve gender parity in media ownership and decision making as well as to give equal voice to women and men; challenge gender stereotypes and ensure balance and sensitivity in all coverage; especially that relating to gender violence.

Out of the 100 media houses approached, 41 answered the institutional questionnaire that provides quantitative data while 18 responded to the perception questionnaire distributed to nearly 200 media practitioners. Those that gave institutional data have a total staff of 10 054 (compared to 11 750 in the 2009 study, and 4 364 in the 2006 study). The sample included 20 print and online media houses; 34 radio; four TV and one TV/radio media houses.

Compared to nine media houses in 2006 and 11 in 2009, the study, funded by the Media Development and Diversity Agency (MDDA), covered a much more diverse range of media than in the past. It included 45 community media; 13 private and one public media house, the South Africa Broadcasting Corporation (SABC). Key findings include:

- **Gender parity is a reality in the overall composition of South African media houses:** At 49% there are equal proportions of women and men in South African media houses compared to the SADC region which recorded 41% women in the media in 2015.
- **Some respondents identified themselves as "other" for the first time:** The other 2% comprises staff who identified themselves as others - (Gender Non-Conforming Persons). This is the first time that this parameter has been measured in the Glass Ceiling Study. The fact that 2% of staff are not identified as male or female is itself an indicator of progress over the last decade.
- **The bigger media houses have all achieved the 50% mark overall:** A total of 24 of the media houses surveyed have between 50%-85% women. The bigger news media in South Africa are in this league of 50% women and above. Media 24 has 57% women, followed by Tiso Black Star (54%); the Mail&Guardian (52%) and the SABC (50%).
- **Increase but still no parity at management level:** Between 2009 and 2018, there has been an increase in women in senior management from 35% to 46% and in top management from 25% to 36%. Women (47%) and men (41%) attributed the gender gap to men being taken more seriously than women. Women (39%) and men (26%) felt that women are by-passed in promotion processes. Women (35%) and men (28%) attributed this to the old boys' network.
- **The proportion of white men in top management has dropped but is still more than double that of white women:** White men, who constituted 46% of top media managers in 2006, have

dropped to 14% in 2018. White women in top management have dropped from 23% to 6% over the same period. But there are still more than double the proportion of white men (14%) to white women (6%) in top management in the media.

- **Black men are moving up the ranks at a much faster pace than black women:** The proportion of black men in top management in the media has more than doubled from 22% in 2006 to 50% in 2018. The proportion of black women in top management has gone up five fold, from 6% in 2006 to 30% in 2018, but this is still 20 percentage points lower than for black men. Black women (30% in top management compared to 46% of the population) are grossly under-represented. The gap is beginning to narrow for black women at senior management level, where they comprise 40% of the total.

- **There has been an increase in women middle managers, but decline in skilled professionals:** Women middle managers such as assistant editors, news presenters/anchors, correspondents, designers and producers have increased from 47% to 52%. However, there has been a decline in women skilled technical and academically qualified workers (such as reporters and sub-editors) from 51% to 38%. This may reflect the general decimation of these core foot soldiers as new media takes over the mainstream media.

- **The gender pay gap appears to be widening:** In the three media houses that provided data, the pay gap between women and men in 2018 at 23% is higher than in 2009 (17%). This may in part reflect the "eroded middle" in which women tend to predominate in the new media era, with the structure of media increasingly dominated by a few top executives, and a large number of junior staff responsible for social media.

- **Policies do not promote equal sharing of responsibilities in the home:** 81% of the media houses said they have maternity leave, compared to only 31% with paternity leave policies.

- **Sexual harassment is a daily reality for women in the media, but is not prioritised:** In 2018, 87% of media houses said they had sexual harassment policies, compared to 82% in 2009. Almost all media houses (91%) reported dealing with sexual harassment cases. Countless first-hand accounts in the report attest to sexist attitudes and practices at work and in the field. The SABC has set up a commission of inquiry into sexual harassment. But respondents agreed that race, growing audiences, reaching new audiences and beating competitors are a much higher priority at the moment than gender.

- **Cyber misogyny is a growing threat:** While only 6% of official respondents felt that cyber misogyny is an issue in South Africa, 30% of women and 9% of men who responded to the perception questionnaire agreed that women journalists do face cyber violence. The first hand account by Ferial Haffajee, a former chair of Sanef, and one of South Africa's most senior women editors, is chilling testimony to one of the ugliest emerging forms of gender violence in the media. Cyber misogyny may just be emerging, but like the speed of the social media that spawned it, is guaranteed to spiral out of control if not addressed seriously.

- **A new breed of young media women are asserting their rights:** The *Glass Ceilings 2018* reflects both a feminist backlash, and an increased anger and assertiveness by women in the media against sexism, which may be the result of the general *zeitgeist* of the times globally and nationally.

- **Key recommendations include:** Greater ownership and control of the media by women, especially black women; all media adopting gender and diversity policies; setting targets for achieving parity at all levels; banning sexism; calling out "mansplaining"; revealing and closing the gender wage gap; opening spaces for women to speak out; family friendly practices; self-monitoring and reporting.

CHAPTER 1

Introduction
Context and Methodology

Participants at the Glass Ceiling inception meeting 2018.   *Photo: Gender Links*

In 2004, Ferial Haffajee became the first woman editor of the *Mail&Guardian*, the first woman editor of a leading newspaper in South African history.[1] Esmaré Weideman became the Chief Executive Officer of Media24 in 2010. She is retiring after eight years at the helm and will be succeeded by Ishmet Davidson, currently CEO of Media24 Print Media[2]. In 2013, Phylicia Oppelt was appointed editor of the Sunday Times, a first in the 107-year history of the paper.[3] These were milestones for women in the media. This was an exception and not the norm. It shows how rare women's top leadership in the media is, nearly 25 years since South Africa's first democratic elections.

The proportion of women in media management does not square with the proportion of female students in journalism and media studies departments. The question that arises is what happens to women in journalism and why do

1 https://allafrica.com/stories/200401260055.html
2 https://www.media24.com/media24-ceo-esmare-weideman-retire/
3 https://www.iol.co.za/news/south-africa/sunday-times-gets-first-female-editor-1462789

they continue to face the proverbial glass ceiling in the media?

As South Africa continues on the road of transformation this transformation should also be reflected in the influence, ownership and control of the media by diverse groups, especially women. Transformation should include changes in work place practices, composition and content. Transformation of the media in South Africa will not be complete if women and men are not given equal opportunity and representation and women still face sexism and discrimination on the basis of their sex. The need for gender equality is firmly anchored in the South African Constitution as well as regional and inter-national women's rights instruments and hence is an important issue when looking at the media.

This chapter outlines the global and regional context; the South African media context; the current realities facing the media, and their gender dimensions. It provides a summary of the methodology and the sample for the research on which the report is based.

Global and regional context

Beijing Declaration and Platform for Action
Twenty-three years ago The Beijing Declaration and Platform for Action (BDPA), an outcome of the 1995 Fourth World Conference on Women, prioritised the media as one of 12 critical areas of concern for the advancement and empowerment of women. The need to advance gender equality in and through the media and information and communications technology (ICT) has been at the core of gender and media advocacy work since that time.

The BDPA has two strategic objectives for the media:

- Strategic objective 1: Increase the participation and access of women to expression and decision-making in and through the media and new technologies of communication.
- Strategic objective 2: Promote a balanced and non-stereotypical portrayal of women in the media.

The BDPA also encourages women's training and adoption of professional guidelines to reduce gender discrimination within the media industry.

This has formed a basis from which media advocacy and policy work has been built over the years and continues to inform research policy work on gender equality in and through the media and ICTs.

The International Steering Committee of the Global Alliance on Media and Gender (GAMAG), an initiative of UNESCO with a network of 500 media organisations and civil society groups around the world, has expressed concern that progress towards media that support gender equality and women's rights objectives remains painfully slow.

"We cannot talk about equality, good governance, freedom of expression and sustainability when women are effectively silenced in and through the media, and where new technologies are used to undermine the human rights of women and women journalists," the committee's then chairperson Colleen Lowe Morna and CEO of Gender Links in South Africa declared at the end of the Committee's inaugural meeting in Geneva in 2015. According to the World Editors Forum's organiser, award-winning Australian journalist Julie Posetti, women worldwide have been waiting for 20 years for real change. "It's 20 years since an historic UN conference in Beijing saw 189 countries adopt the Beijing Declaration and Platform for Action, a visionary roadmap for women's rights and empowerment," she noted in *The Media Online* in August 2015.

The SADC Protocol on Gender and Development

The SADC Protocol on Gender and Development is recognised globally as having some of the strongest provisions in the world on gender equality in and through the media. The Protocol, which was adopted in 2008 and later revised in 2016 alludes to the tenets of the Beijing Declaration in line with the Sustainable Development Goals. The Protocol declares that "State parties shall take measures to promote the equal representation of women and men in the *ownership* (added in 2016), and decision-making structures, of the media. The Protocol encourages the media to give equal voice to women and men in all areas of coverage, including increasing the number of programmes for, by and about women on gender-specific topics that challenge gender stereotypes.

However research shows that "the governance structures of media houses in Southern Africa remain firmly in the hands of men (70%), with women constituting only 30% of those on boards of directors."[4] The Gender and Media Progress Study conducted by Gender Links in 2015 also shows that women make up 40% of total employees[5] in SADC media houses: "in Southern Africa, the media has been largely dominated by men controlling the major institutions and making the decisions in media houses. The lack of women in decision making positions often results in policies that reflect only part of society".[6]

Gender in the media

Research on gender and the media tends to focus on representation and portrayal of women through media content and not so much of the media as an industry in which women are supposed to have equal representation, opportunity, or questioning institutional practices and policies that inform the environment in which women work.

One of the first efforts to ascertain gender in the media work spaces was done through an international study the Unfinished Story: Gender Patterns in Media Employment by Margaret Gallagher which illustrates that between the years 1990-1995 women shared only 33% of media employment in South Africa (Gallagher, 1995:12). By 2000 this figure improved to 42% representation in the media (Goga, 2000). Adding to this wealth of information Gender Links (GL) and SANEF in 2006 carried out a survey that found that amongst other issues that discriminatory practices, structural inequalities, cultural factors, prejudices, patriarchy and sexism are still alive and well in our South African newsrooms. These are clearly prohibiting South Africa's women journalists from realising their potential. The intrinsic "maleness" of the newsroom and journalism practice, a result of a male hegemonic society, is a major cause for women not to be found in senior positions.

Previous Glass Ceiling reports.

In 2009, a survey on 11 media houses carried out by GL whose results were used in the 2011 International Women's Media Foundation (IWMF) *Global Report on the Status of Women in News Media* revealed that women in South African

---

4 SADC protocol Barometer 2017.
5 South Africa not included.
6 SARDC, 2016. SADC Gender and Development Monitor 2016. Tracking progress on Implementation of the SADC Protocol on Gender and Development.

newsrooms constituted 50% of the total. However, women comprised 38% of directors; 35% of senior managers; and 25% of top management: far from this 50% mark. This research seeks to benchmark progress ten years later, within the context of the South African media landscape, and the recent changes in that landscape.

South Africa media context

Media regulation and freedom
The overarching or supreme law that governs everyone and everything is the Constitution of South Africa. It provides for freedom of expression and the right to information but also protects human dignity, and does not allow hate speech or racism, among other undesirables in a progressive society. Here is the exact wording:

The right to freedom of expression is protected by section 16 of the Constitution, which provides that: Everyone has the right to freedom of expression, which includes:
(a) freedom of the press and other media;
(b) freedom to receive or impart information or ideas;
(c) freedom of artistic creativity; and
(d) academic freedom and freedom of scientific research.

This right to freedom of expression does not extend to:
(a) propaganda for war;
(b) incitement of imminent violence;
(c) advocacy of hatred that is based on race, ethnicity, gender or religion, and that constitutes incitement to cause harm.

In terms of media itself, the print sector is governed by co-regulation with The Press Council of SA, which is constituted so that the number of members of the public is higher than the number of members of the media. It also has a retired judge and an Ombudsman as part of the system. However, not all newspapers subscribe to this voluntary system. Independent Newspapers pulled out of The Press Council two years ago (2016) and set up its own Ombudsman, and *The New Age* which briefly became *Afro Voice* before it folded in June 2018, did the same.

It is arguable that changes from self-regulation to co-regulation came about because there was pressure from the ruling party for statutory regulation of the print media via a Media Appeals Tribunal (MAT). The ANC first mooted a MAT at its Polokwane conference in December 2007, and then again at its Mangaung conference, in December 2012. It resolved that there was a need for Parliament to conduct an inquiry on the desirability and feasibility of a MAT, within the framework of the country's Constitution, that is empowered to impose sanctions on the media. Even though an investigation of a tribunal remains a resolution, there was no active pursuit of this in 2018.

Broadcasters are regulated via the Independent Communications Authority of South Africa, and the Broadcasting Complaints Commission of South Africa (BCCSA).

Media freedom trends
Media freedom all over the world is under threat through: violence against journalists, jailing of journalists, politicians' screaming "fake news" at facts which don't suit them, commercial imperatives such as companies putting  the squeeze on the newsrooms when they don't make profits, to a lack of diversity of voices. In August 2018, more than 300 news publications across the US committed to a *Boston Globe* coordinated effort to run editorials promoting the freedom of the press in light of President Donald Trump's frequent attacks on the media, for example calling mainstream media "fake news" and journalists "enemies of the American people".

In South Africa, considering both impending laws and attacks on journalists while on the job, the conclusion reached in this section is this: media freedom in South Africa is under threat, due to the threat of a MAT, the Protection of State Information Bill (dubbed the Secrecy Bill), and of course job losses itself. The Secrecy Bill as well as the resolution for a MAT both have negative implications for the newsroom and journalists. In different ways, these two pieces of proposed legislation would impede the free flow of information, and allow for surveillance of citizens and journalists, by means of tapping phones for example.

Secrecy Bill

In 2018 South Africa received a new president, Cyril Ramaphosa, who said he had to attend to the Bill left on his desk by his predecessor, Jacob Zuma. According to the campaign for the free flow of information, the Right2Know (R2K), the Bill is vague, with ill-defined phrasing that creates space for misinterpretation and overreach.

The definition of "national security matters" is not consistent with international law, and law in other countries, because it included "exposure of economic, scientific or technological secrets", which was too broad, according to the R2K.

The criminal penalties in the law are severe, disproportionate and excessive. Each of the Secrecy Bill offences carries a possible or mandatory prison term of up to five years or a fine for the disclosure and possession of classified information, with a permissible penalty linked to the classification level of the information; up to 25 years imprisonment for the unlawful receipt of state information and for hostile activity offences; and three to 25 years imprisonment for "espionage and related offenses", including a mandatory minimum penalty absent "substantial and compelling circumstances".

There is still no proper public interest defence in the Secrecy Bill: any protection of state information regime should allow "escape valves" to balance ordinary people's rights of access to information and freedom of expression with the state's national security mandate.

Attacks on journalists and intimidation tactics

South Africa's police attacks on journalists appears to be part of a worldwide trend if one considers research by the Committee to Protect Journalists (CPJ), which in 2018 reported a record number of journalists in jail - 262 in 2018, up from 2017, when there were 259.

The worst offenders were Turkey, China and Egypt. The statement also named its global oppressors of press freedom as: the USA's Donald Trump; Recep Tayyip Erdoğan, president of Turkey; Abdel Fattah el-Sisi, president of Egypt; President Xi Jinping, president of China; and Russian president Vladimir Putin, all of whom use rhetoric, and fake news, legal action and censorship to silence their critics.

Journalists in South Africa appear not to be in danger to the same extent, as there are no journalists in jail, for instance. However, there are worrying trends developing. In the past decade in South Africa, photojournalists especially have been targeted by the police and sometimes by protestors, especially when covering demonstrations. They appear to be targeted because of the power of images - photographs can provide incontrovertible proof of events. Anyone with a camera in their cellphone can be a target of police hostility.

There appears to be little evidence that police are adequately trained to understand the role of the media. As a result, women journalists are vulnerable to both police harassment, as well as other forms of harassment in the workplace, as we see from the comments in the chapters to come.

Politics, transformation, regulation and media freedom

The ruling party, the African National Congress' (ANC's) criticism of the print media is that it is a highly concentrated sector which lacks diversity through the entire value chain including ownership and control, race, language, gender, and content. Black ownership, according to the ANC (using the Media Development and Diversity Agency's statistics), is minuscule at 14%,[7] and women's representation at board and management level is 4.44%.[8]

In a nutshell, there is a lack of transformation in the print sector, the party says. To this end, the ANC would like to see more regulation and "accountability" via a Media Charter, for instance.[9]

A Print and Digital Media Transformation Task Team (PDMTTT) was instituted by the industry in August 2012 after Parliament's communication portfolio committee reiterated the need for a Media Charter. Besides a lack of race transformation, according to the Parliamentary committee, there were other charges against the print media: it did not reflect a diversity of South African voices; it marginalised the rural and the poor; it was white-dominated not just in ownership but also in issues covered; and there was "cartel-like behaviour where emergent community and small privately-owned media were smothered through a variety of anti-competitive behaviour".[10] The print media industry was not in favour of a charter at the time.

Pressure continued to mount on the media houses following a resolution taken at the ANC's policy conference in Mangaung in December 2012. The organisation, in its document titled 'Communication and the Battle of Ideas', called for a Media Charter, a Media Appeals Tribunal, an inquiry into print and regulations and an investigation by the Competition Commission into anti-competitive behaviour. The companies felt the industry could be transformed without parliamentary/political or other external intervention.

The PDMTTT was set up in September 2012, under project director Mathatha Tsedu, to develop a common vision and strategy for transformation and to examine, among other issues, the low levels of black ownership in large media groups; lack of diversity; management, control, and employment equity; and skills development. The PDMTTT report noted that women were a mere 1% on boards, and zero percent at the level of media ownership.[11]

The media landscape in South Africa in 2018

Enough is enough: #TotalShutdown March in Johannesburg.
Photo courtesy Marie Claire

The context for the 2018 Glass Ceilings research on women's place in the newsroom and media is one of the huge changes that journalism is experiencing as part of the fourth industrial revolution. It is also done in the context of past

---

7   This figure is disputable, and the evidence of greater black ownership can be seen in the presentations by the media companies to the Print and Digital Media Transformation Task Team (PMDTTT) in the next few pages.

8   See ANC documents: policy conference resolutions about the media at Polokwane, December 2007, and Mangaung, December 2012. ANC document (2010) Media, Transformation, Ownership, and Diversity. www.Anc.org.za/anc-docs/ngccouncil/2010/media http://www.anc.org.za/docs/res/2013/resolutions53r.pdf and finally for the Mangaung policy conference document section Communication and the Battle of Ideas.

9   Ibid.

10 Media release (2012): Launch of the Print and Digital Media Transformation Task Team (PDMTTT), 27 September 2012.

11 PDMTTT (2012) Media release: Launch of the Print and Digital Media Transformation Task Team, 26 September.

reports but the difference in 2018 is a growing militancy and awareness from women about their discrimination, seen in the gender wage gap, the speaking out on cyber bullying and the assertiveness which has come with the global hashtag *#MeToo*, anti-sexual harassment campaign as well as the national *#TotalShutDown* march which took place on 1 August 2018.

The South African newsroom is a tumultuous place today. The media shifts, slides and resists pinning down to a fixed landscape, within which this Glass Ceiling 2018 survey takes place. Traditional media is in decline, and newspapers appear to be in dying faster than expected. The most dramatic change since past Glass Ceilings research is the job loss blood bath in newsrooms.

South Africa very much fits into the global context pattern of traumatic job losses, random and messy digitisation processes, huge downturn advertising revenue to mainstream media and a decline in sales and circulation, according to the global journalism survey, *The New Beats*, which focused on "professional identity transitions", the South African wing of which was recently concluded by Prof Glenda Daniels.

What media do we have in SA?

In 2018, there are between 200-250 newspapers: 16 dailies, 25 weeklies, and over 200 community newspapers. Then there are 360 radio and 556 television stations - including community broadcasters - and an undecided number of online media and digital startups.

The community media sector moves and changes all the time, according to the Association of Independent Publishers (AIP). CEO of the AIP Louise Vale provided the following report in May 2018: "An intensive survey of the sector was completed in May 2016. Print runs and frequency were verified by printing houses across the country and a map and detailed database were produced. This survey indicated that AIP members publish over seven million copies per month reaching, at a conservative estimate, over 20 million readers. It also indicated that 86 members publish in a combination of English, Afrikaans and a local language and that 78% of publications are black owned with 25% owned by women."

The AIP has not conducted an in-depth survey in 2017, but indications are that the sector has taken a hard knock as a result of the downturn in the economy. Independent publishers are the SMMEs of the media sector and it is always the small business that feels the first bite.

Table 1.1: Newspaper circulation in SA 2018 compared to 2014				
	2018	2014	Variance	
Sunday Times	260 132	405 458	-145 326	-36%
Soccer Laduma	252 041	317 013	-64 972	-20%
Daily Sun	141 187	283 216	-142 029	-50%
Rapport	113 636	177 016	-63 380	-36%
Isolezwe	86 342	119 846	-33 504	-28%
The Star	75 836	101 711	-25 875	-25%
Sowetan	70 120	99 403	-29 283	-29%
Isolezwenge Sonto	65 489	93 268	-27 779	-30%
IsolezwengoMgqibelo	64 676			
Son	62 842			
SundaySun	62 674	172 741	-110 067	-64%
DieBurger	61 749			
CityPress	58 566	118 676	-60 110	-51%
Ilanga	56 481	100 853	-44 372	-44%
The Times		142 603		
Sunday World		113 757		

The MarkLives' Biggest Circulation Per Issue Newspaper List* (2018)
*South African paid-for titles only. Comparing to four years ago (2014).

Table 1.1 presents a snapshot of newspaper circulation decline of the biggest circulation newspapers between 2014 and 2018. This shows circulation declines of between 25% and 64% of some of the best known titles such as the Sunday Times, and Daily Sun - where these are still in existence.

Of 204 newspaper titles, publishers of approximate 30 titles are struggling to print regularly, four titles have gone online only, 16 titles have closed completely. Publishers who were publishing more than one title have cut back and are concentrating on one or two titles. The Eastern Cape has been the hardest hit, with an independent group of six newspapers closing after 134 years. At the same time, 17 new publications have joined this year. The AIP is also developing and piloting a hyperlocal news

syndication platform, Takasele http://www.takasele.co.za/ - offering categories titled Everyday, Culture, Womandla, Investigation, Land, Business and Sports.

- Daily newspapers: down from 1 211 887 to 1 051 223, compared to the previous corresponding period.
- Weekly papers: down from 506 730 to 425 204.
- Weekend papers: down from 1 436 844 to 1 306 436.
- Local papers: down from 354 641 to 333 282
- Free papers: down from 6 254 874 to 6 187 758.

Source: http://www.marklives.com/ 2018/05/abc-analysis-q1-2018-the-biggest-circulating-newspapers-in-sa

Besides wide-scale retrenchments, journalists are working twice as hard in newsrooms, juggling more devices to get news out on different platforms, than ever before, according to State of the Newsroom, SA reports (2013, 2014).

State of SA newsrooms

In summary:
- South African newsrooms are hugely pressured environments.
- The digital transition is confusing and messy.
- The political landscape is threatening.
- Technologically the shifts are seismic.
- The traditional models of journalism are outdated.
- The new issues to grapple with are: innovation, sustainability and brand.
- Mobile and social media are centre stage.
- Change is the new stable signifier.
- The identity of journalism has changed.
- The number of women editors has decreased, particularly of black African women editors.
- Women are experiencing online trolling and cyber bullying.
    Source: Wits Journalism Department's State of the Newsroom, SA reports (2013-2017)

Job losses and loss of women's voices
Large waves of retrenchments of journalists have occurred every few years in the last decade as digital news continues to grow. In just one year, for example, in 2014, over 1 000 journalists lost their jobs (*State of the Newsroom*, 2014). In smaller waves, every year retrenchments took place, with 2016 being another big year for job losses from already depleted newsrooms.

According to Tuwani Gumani of Media Workers Association of SA (Mwasa), interviewed this year, Independent Newspapers employed over 6 000 media workers 10 years ago. In 2018 they employed about 1 400. While newsrooms continued to become more juniorised and depleted of experienced staff and institutional memory, newly trained tech savvy "content producers" who can also "do video" replaced them. In conjunction with these massive changes, social media has become intrinsic to the newsroom and "digital first" is now the mantra.

The gender pay gap is on the agenda
This issue is important to re-visit as we scrutinise the Glass Ceiling findings of 2018. One of the differences from past Glass  Ceilings reports is that we are now operating in a climate of more assertiveness about the gender pay gap, globally.

The report titled *Mind the Gap: Uncovering pay disparity in the newsroom* and published by student reporters in the Asian American Journalists Association's Voices programme in 2017, found that some of the biggest newsrooms in the US are paying women and minority staffers significantly less than their male and white counterparts.

In addition, the Independent Association of Publishers' Employees, the union representing many journalists at *The Wall Street Journal*, published an analysis in 2017 showing that women employed by the paper's publisher, Dow Jones & Company, made less than 85 percent what their male counterparts did. That started a larger conversation about pay equity in the industry and prompted other newsroom unions to publish their own studies about pay gaps. The report also said that diversity in newsrooms has been bad for decades and it probably won't get any better.

Social media - the new dimension
The days are over when journalists and editors deal with just editorial - they are now under pressure to be cognisant of the business of media, as the Chinese wall between editorial and advertising has all but collapsed. Journalists are

under the watchful eye of algorithms and analytics, all too aware of the pressures of "traffic" to the online sites accompanying the traditional product.

The pattern of the past five years (2013-2018) is accelerating in news media, which is suffering huge declines in circulation (see Appendix A), downsized newsrooms and digital disruption, characteristic of the Fourth Industrial Revolution, and has no viable revenue model or media innovation in sight.

Google, Facebook and Twitter have captured huge chunks of the media space. They account for one fifth of the global advertising spend, and online advertising, and in 2017 for the first time, this overtook television advertising. This change has resulted in declines in advertising, revenue and circulation. For example, according to ABC in May 2018:

Fake news or lies, political propaganda, and trolling/cyber bullying, especially of women, is on the rise. News is in huge demand but consumers of news are now "platform agnostic" and get news from non-traditional sources, ie. multiple platforms. Loyalty to brands is a thing of the past.

#Cyber Misogyny

In the meantime, a new threat against women has emerged. Posetti has identified **cyber misogyny** as the latest form of overt discrimination against women worldwide. Her research shows that women are more trolled than anyone else. Posetti, who has been studying harassment of journalists in the digital space since 2011, conducted a study of Twitter abuse targeting women journalists in 2017, and found that journalism is the only category where women received more abuse than men, with female journalists and TV news presenters receiving roughly three times as much abuse as their male counterparts.

Also, there may be a feminist backlash, fuelling resistance to transformation in media houses, which may explain why the numbers of women in senior positions is in decline. However, the media is operating in a climate of the #MeToo movement globally, and the #totalshutdown movement nationally, which has seen an increased assertiveness from women about sexism and patriarchal domination.

Again, we ask: is there a backlash against women everywhere in the world, of which South Africa is an example? Cyber misogyny, expressed via online sexual harassment, stalking and threats of violence, is a genuine psychological - and potentially physical - risk to safety of women journalists. It is also a threat to the active participation of women in civil society debate, fostered by news publishers, through online commenting platforms and their social media channels.

Methodology

To date, GL and SANEF have collaborated in two Glass Ceiling reports. The first Glass Ceiling report, launched in August 2006, investigated:

- What are the realities facing women journalists, specifically senior women journalists in South African newsrooms?
- What do they identify as obstacles, and which strategies can be implemented to redress the situation?

Quantitative data gathered to complement the qualitative established:
- The overall proportion of women and men in South African newsrooms.
- Conditions of employment.
- Comparative information on the average earnings of women and men in newsrooms.
- The gender division of labour in newsrooms.
- The gender division of labour in news beats.

- Policies in place for bridging gender gaps such as recruitment, career pathing and workplace policies.

Nine media houses completed the quantitative questionnaire.

The second report (2009) formed part of the *Glass Ceilings: Women and Men in Southern African Media* conducted by GL across the region, and in partnership with SANEF in South Africa. This study focused on the **media houses** not **newsrooms**. In South Africa, the study is based on research carried out with 11 media with a total of 11 750 employees. Researchers conducted in-depth case studies of two media houses and interviewed four journalists/senior managers/editors for their perspectives on the results. A further 24 senior staff responded to perception questionnaires.

Study design

The study is a progress survey with 2009 as a benchmark, since the parameters of the second survey are most directly comparable. The unit of analysis in the study was the media company. The central problem for examination was institutional behaviour in relation to gender equality in staffing, salaries, policies and ICTs.

Sample

Three criteria guided the sample size of the media houses:
- Type of media.
- Balance between print and broadcast in both the commercial and community media based on audience reach.
- Diversity of audiences.

Researchers that were collecting data during this process assisted in refining and identifying media houses operating in different provinces which included both large- and small-scale news companies.

Some of the dominating media companies include:
SABC;
E Media Holding;
Primedia Holdings;
Kagiso;
M&G Limited;
Independent Newspapers;
Tiso Blackstar;
Naspers/Media24;
MSG Africa Investment Holdings;
Daily Maverick;
TNA Media; and
Caxton.

Most of these companies participated in the Glass Ceilings 2018 research.

Mofokana Tsephe and Sinegugu Shibase community media journalists at a reporting GBV workshop in Pretoria.
Photo: Tarisai Nyamweda

Table 1.2: Survey sample for the 2018 Glass Ceiling report					
Media houses	No of Women	No of Men	Total	Type of media	Ownership
Media 24	1899	2513	4412	Print/Online	Private
SABC	1713	1708	3421	Television/Radio	Public
Tiso Black Star Group	511	604	1115	Print/Online	Private
Izwi loMzansi	38	40	78	Radio	Community
Imbokodo FM	27	33	60	Radio	Community
Mail&Guardian	27	30	58	Print/Online	Private
Intokozo FM	35	18	53	Radio	Community
Algoa FM	22	28	50	Radio	Community
Jozi FM	12	9	48	Radio	Community
Vibe FM	30	13	43	Radio	Community
Radio 786 100.4 FM	20	22	42	Radio	Community
Alex News	16	24	40	Print	Community
Alex TV	22	16	39	Television	Community
Radio Turf	18	20	38	Radio	Community
Inkazimulo Newspaper	21	17	38	Print	Community
KZN Community Newspaper	18	18	36	Print	Community
Radio Mafisa	12	20	35	Radio	Community
Mohodi	16	19	35	Radio	Community
Cape Town TV	17	16	33	Television	Community
Eagle Eye News	10	22	32	Print	Community
Sekhukhune	19	11	30	Radio	Community
Aganang FM	15	14	29	Radio	Community
Musina FM	20	9	29	Radio	Community
Phalaborwa FM	18	10	28	Radio	Community
Daily Maverick	10	14	24	Print/Online	Private
Botlokwa Radio	14	8	22	Radio	Community
Bush Radio	8	13	21	Radio	Community
Leboakgomo FM	11	10	21	Radio	Community
Kingfisher FM	9	10	20	Radio	Community
Tubatse FM	6	12	18	Radio	Community

Media houses	No of Women	No of Men	Total	Type of media	Ownership
Nthavela	2	11	13	Print	Community
Greater Tzaneen Community Radio	5	8	13	Radio	Community
Journalismiziko	6	7	13	Online	Community
Gay Radio SA	10	3	13	Radio	Community
Ngoho News	6	5	11	Print	Community
Lepelle Review	6	4	10	Print	Community
Seipone Newspaper	7	3	10	Radio	Community
CUT FM	5	4	9	Radio	Community
Whale Coast 96FM	4	4	8	Radio	Community
Radio-DUT	1	3	4	Radio	Community
Lichvaal Stereo Fm	1	1	2	Radio	Community
Perception only					
E Media Holdings				Television	Private
Masilonyana News				Print	Community
Caxton				Print	Private
Inner City Gazette				Print	Private
Polokwane Observer				Print	Private
The Daily Vox				Print/Online	Private
Independent Newspapers				Print/Online	Private
Valley FM 88.8 / 92.6				Radio	Community
Zebediela FM				Radio	Community
Radio CCFM				Radio	Community
Vaaltar FM				Radio	Community
Rhodes Music Radio				Radio	Community
PUK FM				Radio	Community
Kaya FM				Radio	Private
Ilanga le Theku				Print	Community
Primedia Holdings				Print	Private
Star FM				Radio	Community
Total	**4 667**	**5 354**	**10 054**		

The Glass Ceiling research targeted 100 media houses from public, private and community media. While this was not achieved due to non-response from some media houses, Table two shows that:

- 59 media houses responded; 41 answered the institutional questionnaire that provides quantitative data; the others only responded to the perception questionnaire.
- Those that gave institutional data have a total staff of 10 054.
- The sample comprised 20 print and online media houses; 34 radio; four TV and one TV/radio media houses.
- In terms of ownership, the sample comprised 45 community media; 13 private and one public media (the SABC).

Bestina Magutu interviews Erick Tokoto at Graceland Hair Salon, Braamfontein, South Africa. *Photo: Gender Links*

The sample is a fair representation of the South Africa media landscape in 2018, covering all nine provinces, a diversity of types and ownership, with a particularly strong representation of community media.

Research Questions
The key research questions were:

- How many women and men are in management, board, editorial, finance and human resources departments?
- Has the media improved in the representation of women in different occupational levels of the media?
- Do media have gender policies that they implement?
- Are there deliberate efforts to promote women in media houses?
- Which media houses are performing better than others are?
- Which sector is performing better than the others are?
- What are the gender dimensions of recent developments, notably the digital revolution, on the media?

Research method

The research combines quantitative and qualitative research methods. GL audited the media by taking the numbers as they are and analysing the gender imbalances within the structures of the media with two questionnaires that included a perception questionnaire and an institutional questionnaire.

Quantitative

An in-depth institutional questionnaire was administered to human resources personnel and a perception questionnaire was administered to select individuals in the media houses. Perception questionnaires were administered to at least five people in each media house who occupy different roles. The questionnaire was also shared online with various media employees from different media houses. The questionnaire requested a breakdown of employees by occupational level, conditions of employment earnings, selection and recruitment, workplace practices.

Section one: Occupational levels
This section probes how many women and men there are at the different job levels in the organisation and which races are in these levels. These include top management; senior management; professional staff; skilled technical and academically; semi-skilled and unskilled.

Section two: Conditions of employment
This section looks at how people are employed in terms of their contracts. Whether they in full time open ended contracts; full time fixed term contracts; part time contracts or employed on a freelance or ad hoc basis.

Section three: Earnings
This section seeks to find out if there are pay gaps among women and men in the media houses. In this section the organisation has to provide the earnings of all women and all men working in the media. This will be a sensitive topic but it is very important for the research. Explain to the interviewee that you are not looking for individual salaries but, as group, what women earn and what men earn.

You also need to know how many women in total and how many men in total earn that amount. Once you have that you can average out the earnings by dividing the total earnings of women by the number of women employed and the same for men. This is also done according to what racial group the women and men belong to.

Section four: Categories
This section engages with the different areas of work in the media and the percentage of women in the different categories. These include editorial; presenters; production; design; technical; finance

and administration; advertising /marketing and distribution.

Section five: Selection and recruitment
This section probes if newsrooms have put in place targets to increase the number of women in the newsroom. It starts with 1996; then looks at current figures of 2018. If the organization does not have the figures for the past or targets for the future leave the column blank. If a media house did not exist as at 1996 record the figures for when it began.

Section six: Career pathing
This section looks at mechanisms and strategies in place to assist women in advancing in newsrooms.

Section seven: Workplace policies and practices
This section looks at working hours, employment condition and facilities available to accommodate women's multiple roles. It also seeks to gather information on policies and whether the policies in place promote a more equitable and safe work environment particularly for women.

Section eight: Online media
This section looks at online media dynamics in the media house.

Qualitative

GL compiled case studies that amplify observations drawn from the quantitative analysis. Case studies collected on the experiences of women in the media.

GL and SANEF gathered a total of 201 responses for the perception questionnaires from across 20 media houses. These were filled in by people in different occupational levels as well as departments. The number of institutional questionnaires collected was 47.

Case studies and profiles were gathered to enrich the research with anecdotal evidence.

These included profiles of women in the media who told of their success stories but also stories on sexism and struggles they have in their professional careers.

The quantitative and statistical information from this study are triangulated with the attitudes, perceptions and experiences of men and women to the qualitative aspects of the research.

The rationale is simply that news producers do not work in a vacuum. The creation of an enabling environment to mainstream gender in all aspects of the organisation cuts across all areas in a media house. The commitment to gender equality starts with the vision and mission and clear commitment from management and all staff.

Limitations

Media houses not forthcoming with their data: Initially GL and partners targeted 100 media houses however despite many efforts to engage some of the media houses. However, not all were willing to share their statistics. Some highlighted that the research was not beneficial to them. However, as noted earlier, the study is broadly representative of the South Africa media landscape, with a sample of over 10 000 media employees.

Comparability of the different studies: Because each study builds on the one before it, the parameters are slightly different and not always directly comparable. The sample is also not the same. In 2009, the study gathered quantitative data from 11 media houses, compared to 41 in the current study. However, the majority of these were community radio stations with less than 100 employees. The sample of 10 054 is comparable to the 2009 sample of 11 750. Where comparisons have been made these are between the 2009 and the 2018 study, across similar parameters, providing a span of almost ten years to benchmark progress.

Timeframes: The enormity of this research resulted in the analysis taking longer than initially anticipated.

Making every voice count: An SABC reporter interviews the Centre for the Study of Violence and Reconciliation ahead of the Sixteen Days of Activism on Violence Against Women.
Photo: Colleen Lowe Morna

CHAPTER 2

Women@Work in the Media

Petronella Ngonyama presents on the proportion of women in management in Southern Africa during a SADC Gender Protocol Barometer launch in South Africa.
Photo: Thandokuhle Dlamini

Diversity in media workforce composition remains a critical issue in the sector. Having a diverse media workforce opens the door to equal and better representation of the different communities that make up our country. A diverse workforce must be able to shift what the media prioritises as it reflects and carries different perspectives to news coverage and institutional practices.

Over time, women have made significant progress in gaining access to media, in essence attaining better representation and participation. They have also become aware and are fighting the hurdles that stand in the way of progression into occupying higher levels in the sector.

One overarching reality is that women are underrepresented in key decision-making. This means that generally men continue to dominate the media the world over. According to the Gender and Media Progress Study "women today have a significant presence in the industry, but they continue to struggle to break the glass ceiling and move up the ladder in media houses."[1]

---

[1] Ndlovu and Nyamweda, 2015: Gender and Media Progress Study. Gender Links. Johannesburg.

This chapter begins by exploring why diversity matters in the media. It presents the findings of the study with regard to women's overall representation; their representation in different occupations; how this breaks down by race and sex as well as the gender division of labour in different departmental pursuits. These figures are illuminated with several personal accounts of senior women in the media. The chapter then examines what policies are in place, or need to be in place, to promote gender equality in the media. The conclusions point to the need for policies that go beyond quotas to address underlying systemic issues that result in women failing to break through the proverbial glass ceiling.

Gender diversity in media: why we need it

Women's voices deepen democracy, adding the diversity needed for inclusivity and plurality. As academic and media analyst Julie Reid writes: "The value of a diverse spectrum of media, particularly news media content, is widely recognised as integral, and at times regarded as synonymous, with a well-functioning democracy in which an informed citizenry is actively able to participate."

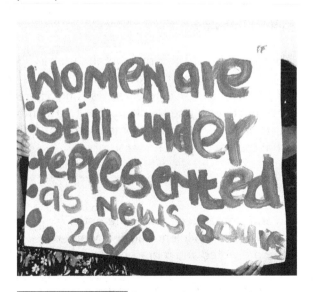

Otherwise, it is just the same old elite talking the same language (with male and white dominating ideologies) to each other. And, as Michele Weldon, assistant professor emerita of Medill School of Journalism, Media, Integrated Marketing Communications in the US and director of Medill Public Thought Leaders notes: "If you have a newsroom that's predominantly male, then the story ideas, source choices and way a story is presented will reflect that point of view. When that happens, you get a skewed view of the world and that's not what the world is like."[2]

According to the International Women's Media Foundation, a glass ceiling is an invisible but real barrier to advancement of women in the workplace, where they can be blocked by sexism, sexist practices, sexual harassment, pregnancy, patriarchal views and prejudices, in hiring and promotions as well as salary disparities with men. There can also be gains and then a "backlash".

In feminist theory, American feminist journalist and author Susan Faludi describes a backlash as also a historical trend, generally recurring when it appears that women have made substantial gains in their efforts to obtain equal rights. It is a counter-assault to halt or reverse the hard-won gains in the quest for equality. British cultural theorist, feminist and commentator Angela McRobbie explains the Faludi backlash as a "concerted, conservative response to the achievements of feminism".

Amanda Gouws, gender researcher and political analyst from Stellenbosch University, argues that women have been experiencing a backlash[3] in all three continents in the global south in the last three years as a consequence of neo liberal capitalism, the overarching global political framework which has not created justice and equality for those on the margins of mainstream politics and economics.

[2] http://www.northwestern.edu/newscenter/stories/2014/02/women-journalists-in-the-newsroom.html#sthash.nlfGUaUk.dpuf
[3] The term backlash gained popularity in 1991 with Susan Faludi's explanation that after gains in feminism there is a backlash from the traditionalists and establishment against such gains.

Number of women editors - does it matter?

Yes, it does matter, says professor Ylva Rodny-Gumede in a 2015 article in *The Journalist* titled 'Women's voices missing discourse'. She writes: "Despite positive developments in terms of achieving racial equity in the newsroom and an increasing awareness of identity and how these impacts on coverage and the stories that journalists work on, dig a little deeper and gender inequities quickly reveal themselves. Many black and female journalists still feel piloted by race and gender and intersections hereof."

Rodny-Gumede says that a survey of 37 journalists and 280 undergraduate journalism students, male and female, at the University of Johannesburg reveals that there is a strong socialisation process favouring male oriented practices as well as news content. "As such, gender differences are quickly overtaken by an ethos that dictates journalistic practices. This is supported by the fact that journalism students, male and female, believe to a higher extent that they can change the news agendas and impact news content, more so than female journalists with two years and more experience from a South African newsroom. The idealism brought into, and often reinforced, through their studies, is seemingly quickly dispelled once entering the newsroom."

Importantly, Rodny-Gumede highlighted in her research that female journalists working in newsrooms would like to have a greater influence on news coverage and the news agenda. "There are also gender differences in how male and female journalists articulate their own role. While male journalists put emphasis on a watchdog role, female journalists put the emphasis on engagement with particular communities, and argue for the news media to open up to previously neglected groups in society. There seems to be a greater awareness as well as willingness among female journalists to recognise marginalised communities, which are to a great extent made up of women and children," she noted.

One of the conclusions of her research is that as we want to believe change has happened, the truth is uncomfortable. "Women do not set or influence news agendas and as such, public discourse formation in South Africa is still dominated by men."

Respondents in all the surveys noted that gender equality would be taken more seriously if women were in senior management positions, and most respondents agreed that female journalists were more likely to seek out female opinion than male journalists were.

However, in 2018, respondents also took a wider view, commenting that gender balance is important because different sexes bring different perspectives in the media house. For the most part, respondents found women had certain gifts that bring value to a newsroom.

"Women have a good way of approaching people."
"Everybody has the same capabilities, but men and women see things differently."
"Women report sensitively on issues pertaining to rape and violence against women and children. There are narratives that are better presented and represented by the concerned gender."
"Different perspectives help a company thrive and avoid becoming stagnant."

As managers, women are perceived as more caring - and more professional. One respondent noted that "it makes a big difference having a CEO who is a woman and who does not suffer fools. Golf and old boys' clubs are scorned. Selections are self-explanatory, no elaboration necessary."

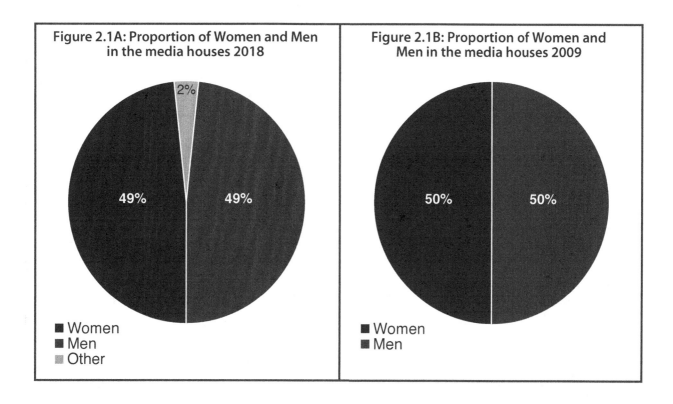

Figure 2.1A: Proportion of Women and Men in the media houses 2018

2%
49%
49%

- Women
- Men
- Other

Figure 2.1B: Proportion of Women and Men in the media houses 2009

50%
50%

- Women
- Men

Figure 2.1A shows that at 49% there are equal proportions of women and men in South African media houses compared to the region which recorded 41% women in the media in 2015. The other 2% comprises staff who identified themselves as others - (Gender Non-Conforming Persons). This is the first time that this parameter has been introduced in the Glass Ceiling Study. The fact that 2% of staff are not identified as male or female is itself an indicator of progress over the last decade.

Figure 2.1B shows the proportion of women and men in South African media houses in the 2009

study. This found that women constituted 50% of the employees in South Africa media houses. Compared to the Southern African region which recorded 41% women in the media, South Africa continues to have a higher proportion of women working in its media sector.

However not all media houses have yet achieved or exceeded the 50% SADC Gender Protocol target for gender parity by 2030. Table 2 shows a breakdown of the proportions of women and men in the media houses that provided data on their employees.

Table 2.1: Women and men by media houses			
Name of Media House	% Women	% Men	% Other[4]
Community media			
Nthavela	85%	15%	
Radio-DUT	75%	25%	
Eagle Eye News	69%	31%	
Tubatse FM	67%	33%	
Bush Radio	62%	38%	
Greater Tzaneen Community Radio	62%	38%	
Alex News	60%	40%	
Radio Mafisa	57%	34%	
Algoa FM	56%	44%	
Imbokodo	55%	45%	
Mohodi	54%	46%	
Radio Turf	53%	47%	
Journalismiziko	54%	46%	
Radio 786 100.4 FM	52%	48%	
Izwi loMzansi	51%	49%	
KZN Community Newspaper	50%	50%	
Kingfisher FM	50%	45%	
Lichvaal Stereo Fm	50%	50%	
Whale Coast 96FM	50%	50%	
Aganang FM	48%	52%	
Cape Town TV	48%	52%	
Leboakgomo FM	48%	52%	
Inkazimulo Newspaper	45%	55%	
Ngoho News	45%	55%	
CUT FM	42%	58%	
Alex TV	41%	56%	
Lepelle Review	40%	60%	
Sekhukhune	37%	63%	
Botlokwa Radio	36%	64%	
Phalaborwa FM	36%	64%	
Intokozo FM	34%	66%	
Musina FM	31%	69%	
Seipone Newspaper	30%	70%	
Vibe FM	30%	70%	
Gay Radio SA	23%	77%	
Jozi FM	19%	25%	56%
Sub total	*50%*	*47%*	*3%*
Private media			
Daily Maverick	58%	42%	
Media 24	57%	43%	
Tiso Black Star Group	54%	46%	
Mail&Guardian	52%	47%	
Sub-total	*44%*	*56%*	
Public media			
South African Broadcasting Corporation	50%	50%	
Sub-total	*50%*	*50%*	
Total	**49%**	**49%**	**2%**

[4] Recordings of "other" in most media houses were too small to be recorded as a %.

As illustrated in Table 2.1, the proportion of women in the media ranges from 19% (Jozi FM, which also had the highest proportion of other) to 85% women in Nthavela, a community media station. A total of 24 of the media houses surveyed have between 50% -85% women. The bigger news media in South Africa are in this league of 50% women and above. Media 24 has 57% women, followed by Tiso Black Star (54%); the Mail&Guardian (52%) and the SABC 50%.

Table 2.2: Comparative analysis of women in select media houses 2009 and 2018			
Media house	Proportion women 2018	Proportion women 2009	Variance
SABC	50%	60%	-10%
Mail&Guardian	52%	55%	-3%
Media 24	57%	46%	+11%
Leboakgomo FM	48%	42%	+6%

Comparing figures for individual media houses (where such data exists) between the 2009 and 2018 Glass Ceiling studies shows that the SABC and Mail & Guardian registered declines, but are still above 50%. Media 24 showed the most dramatic increase, from 46% to 57%, and 11 percentage point increase. Media 24 had its first woman CEO (Esmaré Weideman) - one of the few women in such a position - for most of this period. The proportion of women at Leboakgomo FM increased by six percentage points (from 42% to 48%).

Some respondents in the survey noted that they continue to face challenges in getting women in their media houses. Some noted challenges in attracting and maintaining staff on the salaries they offer especially in the commu-nity media sector. They manage to achieve their targets by employing fairly young people and training them on the job. Some media houses such as Bush Radio noted that they have managed to reach these targets because they have a 50/50 policy on recruitment.

Proportion of women and men by ownership
Figure 2.2 shows that the private media (56%) has the highest proportion of women, followed by public media (50%) and community media (also 50%). Community media had the highest

proportion of Gender Non-Conforming Persons (3%).

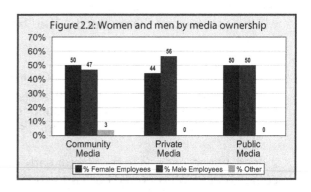

Figure 2.2: Women and men by media ownership

Proportion of women and men by medium

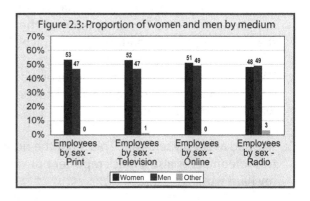

Figure 2.3: Proportion of women and men by medium

An analysis by medium (Figure 2.3) shows that there is a higher proportion of women in the print media (53%), in television (52%) and online media (51%) compared to radio. Only in the radio sector does the proportion of men (49%) surpass that of women (48%). However at 3%, this sector has the highest proportion of Gender Non-Conforming Persons. Race remains a factor for women especially in broadcasting, as reflected in the case study that follows:

When you have the 'wrong' accent

"As you can tell, my accent is not one of those 'Model C' ones. I attended public schools," says **Busisiwe Ntuli**, executive producer of *Special Assignment*, as she recounts her 16-year journey in the media industry.

That throw-away comment underscores the battles black journalists face in South Africa. Ntuli's social background was already a "negative" even before she commenced her work career.

Ntuli cut her teeth in journalism at the *Sowetan* where she did her short internship, but later decided to go and study for a journalism degree after completing a short course in the subject. Soon afterwards, she joined the Johnnic Pearson Financial Journalism internship programme. Johnnic Communications, which was to become the present day Tiso Blackstar group, owned Summit TV, today known as Business Day TV.

On graduating, the interns would be placed in one of the subsidiaries: the TV station and one or another of the publications. "Even as an intern, I learnt quickly that your accent determined the pace of your growth, which direction you were headed to, and also the treatment you were likely to get from the people you encountered at the company," says Ntuli.

Indeed, her accent was to be a factor early on in her career, which would lead to her removal from completing a high-powered business assignment "because that voice is not suitable for an important story like this... " And that "story" was the JSE listing of state-owned company Telkom for Summit TV.

"It was exciting to be involved in a hard-core business project. I was at the JSE offices in Sandton early in the morning. After the completion of the function, I prepared my story, packaged it and put it on the system (for later broadcast), after which I left.

"While at home, I received a call from one of my colleagues telling me that my story had been taken from me and given to someone else. That decision was apparently taken by Gary Alfonso, who I think was the managing editor.

"He had allegedly said that 'This is not the right accent for such an important story'. He gave the story to someone else, also a black reporter but with a private education accent. I was not given credit for my hard work."

At the next day's diary session, Ntuli raised the issue of the story. Some of her colleagues backed her up. "I was furious," she says. "I demanded an apology from Gary, but he refused to apologise. That demand for an apology was regarded by Gary as a declaration of war. He made sure that he was going to get rid of me. He wanted to show me who the boss was."

The incident of an accent, which led to the fallout, was to precipitate the parting of ways between Johnnic Communications and Ntuli. She moved on to the SABC's newly-established business news programmes. In 2007, she joined *Special Assignment* as a documentary producer. When Ntuli was appointed as executive producer of Special Assignment - the first black woman to occupy such a position - there were those who would challenge her authority.

There were comments such as, "I am a CNN award-winning journalist with more than 20 years' experience in this game, what can you tell me"? And "we need a strong man with a no-nonsense attitude to lead us".

"This behaviour and attitude by some subordinates," she says, "can only be ascribed to the fact that I am a black woman occupying a senior position, previously associated with white males and females."

Women in different occupational categories

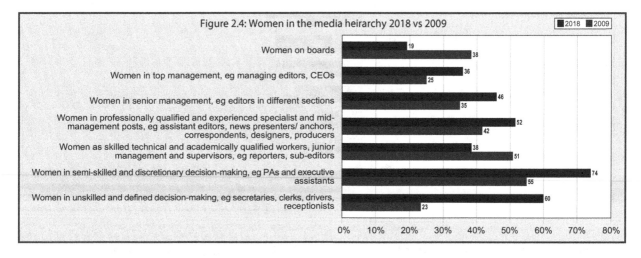

Figure 2.4: Women in the media heirarchy 2018 vs 2009

Figure 2.4 shows that between 2009 and 2018, there has been an increase in women in senior management from 35% to 46% and in top management from 25% to 36%. This suggests that women are increasingly making strides in the sector and breaking the glass ceiling, occupying previously male dominated echelons in the media. However in as much as they occupy top and senior management the proportion of women in media is now half of what is was in 2009. The decline in the proportion of women on boards from 38% in 2009 to 19% in 2018 is also a concern.

At the middle level, there has been an increase in women middle managers (such as assistant editors, news presenters/anchors, correspondents, designers and producers) from 47% to 52%. However, there has been a decline in women as skilled technical and academically qualified workers (such as reporters and sub-editors) from 51% to 38%. This may reflect the general decimation of these core foot soldiers as new media takes over the mainstream media (see introductory chapter).

There has been an increase in the proportion of women in the unskilled and semi-skilled categories: from 23% to 60% and 55% to 74% respectively. These are the lower paid categories. One area in which men are likely to have been losing jobs as a result of the shift to online media and decline in circulation figures is as drivers. This would push up the proportion of women in these categories, without necessarily increasing the absolute numbers.

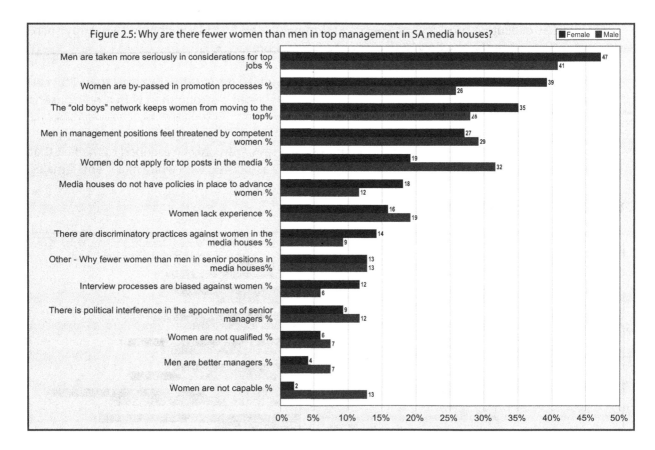

Figure 2.5: Why are there fewer women than men in top management in SA media houses?

Figure 2.5 summarises perceptions by women and men on why there are fewer women than men in top jobs in the media. The majority of women and men attributed this to unseen and unspoken discriminatory attitudes and practices rather than deliberate policies or capability.

The top reason given by women (47%) and men (41%) said that men are taken more seriously. Women (39%) and men (26%) felt that women are by-passed in promotion processes. Women (35%) and men (28%) attributed this to the old boys' network. Much lower proportions of women and men said that women lack experience (19% women, 16% men) or that women are not as qualified (6% women and 7% men). It is telling however that the biggest divergence between women and men was on whether women apply for media jobs, with 32% men maintaining they do not, compared to just 19% women. Also of concern is the fact that 13% men (compared to 2% women) maintained that women are not capable. In the case study that follows, veteran broadcaster Portia Kobue reflects on the intricate interplay between editorial control and gender during her years at the public broadcaster.

Appointed to take the blame ?

Women are often offered top jobs but given little authority, according to **Portia Kobue**, currently the news editor at Kaya FM, formally executive producer for *Morning Live* and later head of *Interface*, a discussion and analysis programme on the SABC.

"The belief - unspoken as it was - was that female executives were easy to manipulate, and could be prevailed upon to agree to broadcast material that more often than not was weighted towards a political objective and agenda, and which might not have been agreed to at the day's news diary," she reflects. Curiously though, the SABC tended to have more women executive producers than males. The executive producer is responsible for the final product that is broadcast to the public.

By appointing women into these positions, the "heavyweights" - mostly men - are protected from blame in the event that something is broadcast that did not sit well with political bosses. It has to be pointed out that male reporters at equivalent level were also subjected to bullying. However, in their case they tended to come together (with the bullies) in some form of a "boys' club" while women were regarded as outsiders.

The political heavyweights saw nothing wrong with interfering with editorial policy, and according to Kobue, a general manager of news once told her "that policy does not work here. You must listen to instructions. On the contrary he pleaded, not instructed me to 'cooperate and help him out' - presumably so that he wouldn't get into trouble if I refused to toe the line," she says.

In her presentation to the SABC-appointed Commission on Editorial Policy, Kobue makes startling allegations. Amongst these is when she met a former head of television news along the corridor. He wanted to know why there hadn't been any coverage of the president (at the time Thabo Mbeki). "He continued, *'ka-mopresidente waka ke bolaya motho'* (I will kill someone when people mess up with my president)," says Kobue.

"I was under immense pressure to accommodate ANC and government officials. They regarded the public broadcaster as their property and expected us to bow to their demands and instructions." Kobue cites a number of incidents that had the effect of undermining her authority. At one point, after she and her team had finalised and agreed on the day's diary, "out of nowhere, a senior government official walked into our office, apparently waiting to be interviewed without my knowledge or involvement in scheduling the interview.

"When I questioned what was happening, I was told that the head of news and current affairs had made the arrangements for the official to come in for an interview. This was done without even consulting me.

"I would receive a call from the spokesperson of a former minister of foreign affairs instructing me to send a team to cover the minister as she was leaving on African Union business, or would ask me to record a statement which he read out. This would happen in the middle of a broadcast when I was expected to be concentrating on the screen," says Kobue.

"Sexist and inappropriate language was routinely used by men to refer to women or to make sexually explicit comments," she added. "My impression was that sometimes men found it difficult to separate a woman's professional profile from their personal ones. To them women were objects of desire and were there for their gratification."

Race and gender

As the 2009 Glass Ceiling covered the Southern Africa region, it did not disaggregate data by sex since this is not a major consideration in the rest of the region. However, the 2006 study and the 2018 studies did disaggregate data by race and gender. The two samples are not directly comparable, since the 2006 comprised a sample of 4 364 employees, compared to the 2018 sample of 10 054. However, both samples have three sizeable and influential media houses in common: the SABC, Media 24 and the Mail& Guardian. While the samples are not directly comparable, they are indicative. The longer 12 year time span is also useful for measuring change of this kind.

has more than doubled from 22% in 2006 to 50% in 2018. The proportion of black women in top management has gone up five fold, from 6% in 2006 to 30% in 2018, but this is still 20 percentage points lower than for black men.

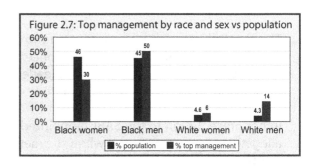

Figure 2.7: Top management by race and sex vs population

Figure 2.7 compares the proportion of women and men by race to their representation in the general population. The white population of South Africa is about 9% of the total, and there is a slightly higher proportion of women than men. Black in this case refers to persons of African, Indian and mixed race origin (91% of the population). Black women constitute 46% of the total population, compared to black men who comprise 45% of the population. The graph shows that while black men, white men and white women are all slightly over-represented in top management, black women (30% in top management compared to 46% of the population) are grossly under-represented.

Figure 2.6: Top management by race and sex 2006 vs 2018

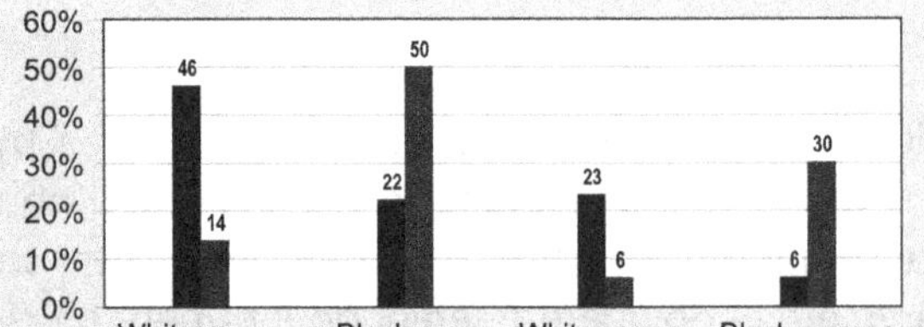

Figure 2.6 points to some dramatic changes at the top management level. The proportion of white men at top management level in the media has gone down from 46% in 2006 to 14% in 2018 and for white women from 23% to 6% over the same period. On the other hand the proportion of black men in top management in the media

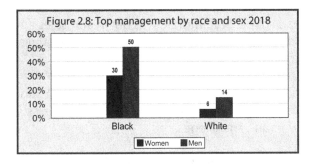

Figure 2.8: Top management by race and sex 2018

Figure 2.8 shows the gender gap by race. It shows that with 50% black men in top management compared to 30% black women, there are 40% more black men in top management in the media than there are black women. There are more than double the proportion of white men (14%) to white women (6%) in top management in the media.

Figure 2.9 reflects the representation of women and men by race in *senior* as opposed to *top* management relative to their representation in the population overall. This shows that while white men (10% in senior management, compared to 4.3% of the population) are still over-represented, the gaps are narrower than at top management level. In particular, the gap at this level is beginning to narrow for black women (40% in senior management, and 46% in the population overall). The concerted push that needs to take place is from senior to top management. The case study that follows is about an up and coming young woman who has made it to top media management and is advocating for greater black *ownership* of the media.

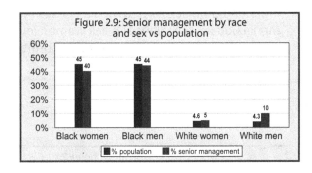

Figure 2.9: Senior management by race and sex vs population

Young, gifted and black

If there were to be a search to find Nina Simone's aspirational young person as proclaimed in her afro-classic song, *To be Young Gifted and Black*, **Verashni Pillay** would sail through that contest with little difficulty.

By her own acknowledgment, Pillay has had a particularly rapid rise in the newsroom over a short space of time. She launched her career at News24 following the completion of her studies at Rhodes University.

Her main responsibilities involved doing original digital reporting for the first time at the publication, an area that appears to be her forte. After completing her two-year service agreement with Media24, she moved over and joined the *Mail & Guardian*, "an organisation I had always wanted to work for", working again in digital reporting.

Soon she was appointed deputy editor of the Mail&Guardian Online. She would move on to become associate editor of the entire title. She took a break and travelled. Coming back in 2015 she was appointed editor-in-chief. At age 31 she became the youngest woman ever - let alone a black one - to be appointed to the highly sought-after position.

"At the time of my appointment the paper was in a bad shape. Staff morale was down and sales and circulation had plummeted. Things were just not looking good," says Pillay. She managed to stabilise the situation, grow circulation, and in the process recruited young blood.

But a falling out over an editorial apology for a factual error led to a coterie of individuals suggesting that the mistakes (with the article) "happened because of inexperience due to her age". The age issue was used as a proxy "to talk about me being a black woman", she alleges.

Pillay was head-hunted to take over as editor-in-chief of online publisher, the *Huffington Post (SA)* where she confronted professional disagreements over the need to beef up sub-editing capacity with undertones of race and gender.

She is currently editor of digital reporting at Power 98.7. Verashni decries the limited number of independent black-owned media houses in the country. Without sufficient numbers of black-owned media houses, the talent of black women journalists will continue to be sidelined, for too much of the current mainstream media is not transformed at an ownership level, she says.

Gender division of labour

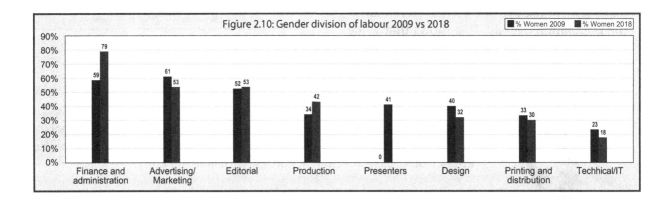

The gender division of labour between women and men across departments continues. Figure 2.10 shows that as in 2009, the highest proportion of women are in finance and administration (79%). This is a 20 percentage point increase on 2009 (59%) possibly due to the decline in the number of drivers commented on earlier.

Women also dominate in the advertising and the marketing departments - 53% in 2018, compared to 61% in 2009. At 52% in 2009, and 53% in 2018, women are still in the slight majority in the editorial department. Women are less than 50% in production (42%, although this is an increase from 34% in 2009); as presenters (41%); in design (40%); printing and distribution (30%) and in technical IT where the proportion of women has dropped from 23% in 2009 to 18% in 2018.

The respondents in the institutional survey noted that the lines between different tasks in media houses are increasingly blurred as a result of budget and staff costs. For instance presenters also act as the producers of the shows they produce. The publisher of the community newspaper also works in distribution.

Policies for achieving gender balance in newsrooms

The workplace practices are often moulded by the policies that are in place to encourage gender equality. Respondents indicated the kind of policies the media houses had put in place to support gender equality in their contexts.

Student journalists from Wits Vuvuzela taking pictures.   *Photo: Dinesh Balliah*

Table 2.3: Policy indicators on fast tracking gender in the workplace			
Workplace indicators	**2018%**	**2009%**	**Variance**
Targeting women	72%	36%	36%
Gender balanced interview panels	81%	64%	17%
Fast tracking policy	25%	18%	7%
Gender considered in succession planning	42%	45%	-3%

Table 2.3 shows that compared to 2009, there have been improvements in policy interventions to increase women's representation in all areas and at all levels of media practice. 72% of respondents in 2018 said their companies target women, compared to 36% in 2009. In 2018, 81% of respondents said that their companies have gender balanced interview panels, compared to 64% in 2009. Although at 25% the proportion who said that their companies have fast tracking policies for women is higher than the 18% in 2009, this is still not high enough, given the glass ceilings that women face in newsrooms. There is also a slight decline, (from 45% to 42%) in those who said that gender is considered in succession planning. These figures go some way in explaining the absence of women from top media posts.

Quotas

Table 2.4: Views on quotas 2018 vs 2009				
	Women		Men	
	2018- %	2009- %	2018- %	2009- %
Quotas are unfair	19	47	12	17
Quotas are fair	20	33	10	50
Quotas should for a limited time	3	0	3	0

As reflected in Table 2.3, the 2018 survey shows considerable ambivalence towards the use of quotas to correct gender imbalances. On the one hand, a much lower proportion of women (19% compared to 47% in 2009) feel that quotas are unfair. The proportion of men who say quotas are unfair also declined from 17% to 12%.

 "Correcting structural imbalances cannot be left to the goodwill of men and women."
"Men's privileged positions have been established over a long period of time. Quotas will accelerate transformation."
"Historical bias and social conditioning cannot be undone without concentrated efforts."

Yet a lower proportion of women (20% in 2018 compared to 33% in 2009) felt that quotas are fair. The decline in the proportion of men who believe that quotas are fair is even greater (from 50% in 2009 to 10% in 2018). "I don't like quotas. They create a negative environment," wrote one respondent. "It is people's outlook on life and how they regard women that should change," said another. The spectre of incompetence also entered the conversation in 2018.

 "Quotas are fine as long as they do not result in placing incompetent people in roles."

Some respondents believed quotas would be acceptable, but with a time limit. "Quotas should be used only to correct the current imbalance. Thereafter a better or fairer strategy should be used that allows for the advancement of both male and female employees," said one respondent.

Conclusions

As in 2009, this chapter shows that the issue in South African media houses is no longer about women's overall representation in the media, but rather their participation at management level, and in different areas of media practice.

While there has been an increase in women's representation at senior and top management, this still falls short of the 50% mark. Women's representation at board level has decreased.

The dramatic increase in the representation of black men in media decision-making is not reflected among black women media practitioners. The double burden of race and gender is real in newsrooms, as attested to by the first-hand accounts quoted in this chapter.

With regard to occupational areas of work, women predominate in administration, finance and marketing. They hold their own with men in marketing. But their numbers decline significantly in production, printing, distribution and the IT/technical fields. This is a reminder that the gender distribution of labour in the world of work is reflected in media houses. Gender benders are still not the norm.

As before, women and men in the media recognise the value of quotas, but they do not see these as a panacea. As demonstrated in the chapters that follow, systemic change is needed to ensure that women have equal opportunities and outcomes in the media.

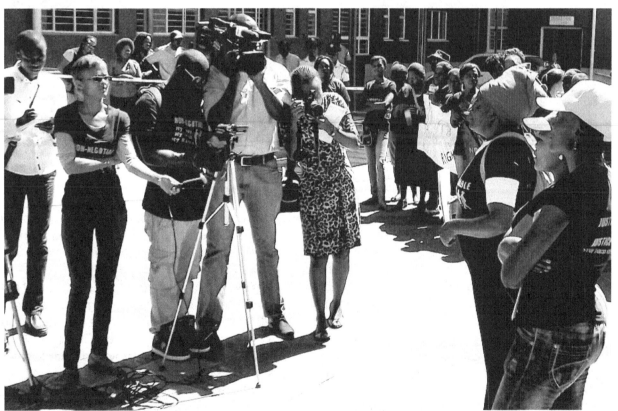

Women@Work in the media.

Photo: Gender Links

CHAPTER 3

The Gender Pay Gap

Nonhle Skosana, content producer at Power 98.7, speaking at a media webinar in Johannesburg.

Photo: Thandokuhle Dlamini

T he gender pay gap is a concrete, measurable indicator of sexism but human resources departments of media companies prefer to hide it. Journalists in the South African newsroom and media companies do not seem to know what the gender wage gap is, but they know it exists.

Despite the media calling for transparency in public affairs, particularly with regard to money, the media itself is less than transparent in sharing wage data. The ask is simple: total earnings for men, divided by number of men, and total earnings for women, divided by number of women. Every human resource department has this information at the click of a button.

Yet every Glass Ceiling study, GL and Sanef have struggled to get sex disaggregated wage data. 2018 was no exception. Despite repeated efforts, only three media houses - Jozi FM, Media 24 and Tiso Black Star Group - provided reliable data. It is especially unfortunate that the SABC - the public broadcaster - did not fill out this part of the questionnaire.

While it is only possible to draw conclusions based on those who responded (that are indicative but cannot be generalised to the whole media) this chapter has been kept as a stand-alone chapter for several reasons. The gender wage gap is on the global agenda, especially in the media.

It is the most telling indicator of the disparities that still exist in the media. It encapsulates where women are in the media hierarchy, as well as the different occupational areas of media work. It raises issues about conditions of service, and what the media is doing to create family-friendly work environments. Most importantly it cries out to the media to walk the talk of transparency! Sanef and GL hope that among others this chapter will encourage other media houses to calculate their gender wage gap, and share it in future studies.

The chapter begins with an overview of the global context, moving to conditions of service, to an analysis of existing data on the gender wage gap. The chapter also examines the extent to which HR policies and practices recognise the dual roles that women often play at work and at home, and what is being done to promote family friendly practices.

The global context

In 2017, the BBC conducted the first big study into the gender pay gap surveying 10 000 big companies and found that 78% of the companies paid men more than women; fewer than one in seven paid women more than men; men make up the majority of higher paid jobs; men are also paid higher bonuses than women. They found there is no sector that pays women more; in some instances men were paid 50% more than women, or twice as much.

The BBC's investigation into itself found a similar gap, that only a third of its top 96 earners were women, and the top seven are all men, according to an article in *The Guardian* in July 2017, titled *BBC facing backlash from female stars after gender pay gap revealed*.

However, by July 2018, the BBC reduced the gender pay gap to 8.4%, according to a follow up article in *The Guardian* in July 2018. The research also showed how different media companies were the more conservative, the bigger the wage gap - for example, *The Telegraph*'s wage gap was 35% and *The Guardian*'s was 11.3%.

The corporation said the main reason for its gender pay gap was that it had too few women in senior leadership roles and more women than men in the lowest-earning part of the workforce, such as administrative staff.

Conditions of employment

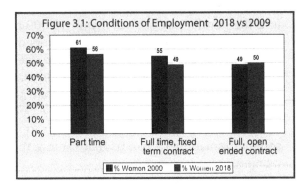

Figure 3.1: Conditions of Employment 2018 vs 2009

Fig 3.1 shows the conditions of employment for women in the surveyed media houses for 2018 compared to 2009. The most secure form of employment is the full time open ended contract. The proportion of women relative to men on part time contracts in the media has decreased from 61% to 56%. But the reality is that more women than men are on part time contracts. Also worrying is the fact that the proportion of women in full time, fixed term contracts has dropped from 55% to 49%. A roughly equal proportion of women (49% in 2009 and 50% in 2018) are on full, open ended contracts.

Qualitative data collected shows that conditions of employment differ across media houses and that several issues influence the type of contracts that women and men get. For instance, one media house noted that it seems the numbers skew towards men because most of the work is at night, even in the middle of the night, so even though they try to recruit women safety can sometimes be an issue that holds them back.

Another noted that women generally prefer to be co-ordinators or presenters, hence numbers are skewed towards men. They noted that this is a phenomenon they are aware of and working on, but it is not an easy thing to change because it is a societal not organisational issue.

Mind the gap!

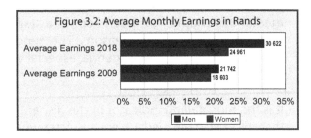

Figure 3.2: Average Monthly Earnings in Rands

In 2009, 11 media houses shared data on wages, compared to three in 2018. The latter comprised two private and one community media house. The findings for 2018 are thus only indicative, but still worth examining. As is to be expected given inflation over the ten-year period, the average earnings of men in the media houses surveyed have risen from R21 498 in 2009 per month to R30 622 per month in 2018, while those for women have risen from an average of R18 395 to R24 961 over the same period. *What is significant is that rather than reducing, the wage gap between women and men appears to be increasing.*

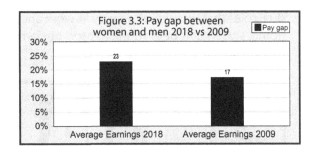

Figure 3.3: Pay gap between women and men 2018 vs 2009

Figure 3.3 shows that among the media houses surveyed, the pay gap between women and men in 2018 at 23% is higher than in 2009 (17%). This may in part reflect the "eroded middle" in which women tend to predominate in the new media era, with the structure of media increasingly dominated by a few top executives, and a large number of junior staff responsible for social media.

Table 3.1: Pay gap by media house			
Media house	Women	Men	% Difference - Women and Men
Average Earnings 2009	18 603	21 742	17%
Media 24	29 438	33 133	13%
Tiso Black Star	37 457	45 233	21%
Jozi FM	7 986	13 500	69%

Table 3.1 provides the wage breakdown for the media houses that were open enough to share their data. This shows that there are variations in the gender wage gap between media houses, from 13% in Media 24 (which has had a woman CEO for the last decade) to 21% in Tiso Black Star to 69% in Jozi FM. Some of the drivers of the gender gaps noted by respondents included the size and scope of the title on which each person works, job level, performance and years of experience.

Salary disparities

The difference in average salaries is explained by a complex web of structural factors. Nearly 80% (157 out of 202) of respondents also claimed that there are still cases of women with the same qualifications and experience earning less than men.

The comments section amplifies this:

"An ex colleague told me his salary, and it was R2 000 more than mine for doing the same job. There might have been other circumstances that led to his salary being higher but it was something I noted nonetheless."

"I once discovered I got paid way less than a male colleague who started at the same time as me, even though I had more qualifications than him. He said it's because he had two more years' experience than me."

"Currently there's a case in SABC Digital News of two women who are earning way less than their male colleagues."

Promotion

As in the previous Glass Ceiling research, most respondents in 2018 feel that men are still taken more seriously for promotion. Women are also seen to fail in demanding recognition and pushing for promotion. However in 2018, only 24% of women said that women are their own worst enemies.

In 2006, one respondent said: "I believe that women partly impose the glass ceiling on themselves by not pushing boundaries. Most women tend to be wallflowers regarding their careers; they expect people will just notice their dedication and hard work. Men learn very quickly about the value of networking and being vocal about their ambitions." Has this changed much in 2018? "I never applied for senior positions until I was asked why I was not applying," said one respondent.

Ironically adding to this reticence is the stigma attached to advancement policies for women.

"Some women don't participate because they do not want to be seen as quota appointments," said one respondent. Once women rise to the top, problems often surface. Some men refuse to take orders from a woman. But dealing with junior women can add another dimension.

 "I am often not taken seriously by my staff. There is no problem with the men but the women don't want to be held accountable by another woman. They expect constant concessions for not going out to cover stories which is sometimes unreasonable. This means more pressure is put on the male reporters to cover stories that require them to go out on the field. The female journalists prefer to sit in the office."

That's one side of the argument. The other is that once women climb the ladder to high position, they pull the ladder up after them:

"Very senior women often pull down younger women, trip them up or otherwise make life hard for them," writes one respondent. "Men often act as the best mentors."

While policies and programmes to assist women staffers may be present within the various employment manuals of most of the large media houses, the manuals are where these end up. The policies and programmes hardly ever get looked at within the newsrooms themselves, the very places for which they were designed.

At best "remedial" measures - where they exist - to right the wrongs of the past, particularly in the area of newsroom gender inequalities, may be said to have missed their target by the proverbial mile. In the case study that follows, a woman journalist argues that female journalists are fighting the same battles fought by their forebears in the fifties.

"It is a lie to say that when you work diligently hard you will be rewarded with promotion" says Monica Laganparsad, the news editor of New Frame, a non-profit organisation that is running a social justice media project which is pro-working class and pro-poor. " At least this does not apply to most women in our newsrooms, and certainly not when you're a black woman."

That kind of observation, coming as it does from someone who has seen it all during her lengthy stay in newsrooms, would make anyone, even the most optimistic among us, sit up and take note.

With over 20 years' experience as a reporter with the country's major media houses, the furthest that Laganparsad could point to by way of advancement was as a middle level reporter, bar a short stint - a year to be exact - when she was appointed deputy news editor at *News24*.

Laganparsad began her career as a freelance journalist in Durban. After proving herself as a writer, she was offered a permanent post at the *Daily News*. For the next seven years Laganparsad covered all imaginable news beats one can find in a newsroom.

On realising that she had reached what was possibly a ceiling (for her) at the Daily News, Laganparsad moved over and joined the national-oriented and mass-circulating *Sunday Times*.

A hardworking go-getter eager to grow her career, Laganparsad was rewarded when she was transferred to Johannesburg where, it was hoped, she would better utilise her reporting skills in an environment that offered wide-ranging and varied reporting possibilities and an enhanced scope for growth.

"I was happy and excited at the prospects that awaited me, knowing that I was now getting exposed nationally and writing about national issues as opposed to regional news. When I got to Johannesburg, I discovered that the newspaper's investigating team was all female. This was good, I thought to myself.

"However, my excitement was short-lived. Not long after my arrival the team was changed to all male." Laganparsad is quick to point out that she does not question the capability and excellent writing skills of some of those who were elevated to become the new investigating team. It was the way it was conducted. It was as if the women had committed a cardinal sin.

"I mean, of that female team, not one was retained, nor was there any effort made to bring on board a different woman at the very least." Against this setback and background, Laganparsad decries the fact that, generally, newsroom executives - editors and news editors, male in the main - do not bother to train their female counterparts.

Training

In 2006, women wanted workshops in which they could be empowered to believe in themselves. Career planning and opportunities to expose them to all kinds of experiences would prepare them for leadership. And they wanted women as role models.

"Women are not empowered and mentored to believe in themselves, that they can fill a senior position, because women also buy into the perception that they cannot compete with men, cannot be as good as men, etc, when they in fact can do things better than men. "

In 2018, things have improved on several fronts. More and more women are enrolling for journalism degrees.

"Not only are the majority of my supervisors and colleagues women, but while I was studying journalism our classes were overwhelmingly female at both an undergraduate and post-graduate level."

Several respondents also mentioned the importance of mentoring. And there was a call for gender forums, as well as training for women to mitigate the risks associated with journalism - everything from physical encounters to trolls. Better training could mean better chances of advancement, rising through the ranks - and earning better salaries. Pay, noted one respondent, "relates mostly to seniority, which is male dominant".

'Family penalty' still a reality

Is the woman's place in the home? Must family come first for women, but not for men? In 2006, one senior journalist said this: "Journalism is 24/7 work and workplaces do not take account of the impact on family responsibility. I don't know, for example, if I could do this work if I had children. There is a lot of external work: interviews, functions, travel, etc that are intrinsic."

Having a family need not limit a woman's rise in the news environment if there are structures in place to support her. But "once a woman becomes a mother there is very little done to accommodate her. There is no accom-modation of a woman who needs a flexible working day - not a shorter day, just a more flexible one. "

"Many women are single parents and have to take care of a full life at home with children, while the majority of men do not have those obligations."

In 2018, it's been described as the 'family penalty', and respondents said it was one of the biggest issues that women face. Women who fall pregnant, or have a number of responsibilities outside the workplace, raising children, etc, often suffer professionally and are less likely to be employed or promoted than men, who are not expected to carry the same burden in their personal lives.

 "We have capable women who can occupy top positions but they are bypassed. There is still a problem of perception - women take maternity leave, women have emotional issues, women can't/won't work long hours because of family responsibilities, women should be at home looking after children."

However, the situation in some media houses has improved since the first survey in 2006. In an unnamed media house, the work environment was described as sensitive to the needs of women, with flexible working arrangements to support a work-life balance, e.g. time for family commitments, gym, or study.

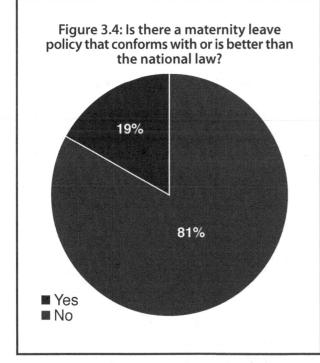

Figure 3.4: Is there a maternity leave policy that conforms with or is better than the national law?

- 19%
- 81%
- Yes
- No

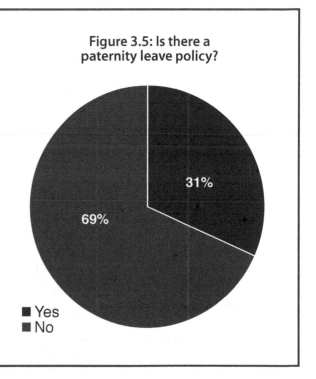

Figure 3.5: Is there a paternity leave policy?

- 31%
- 69%
- Yes
- No

As reflected in figure 3.4, 81% of media houses said they have maternity leave policies that conform with or are better than the national law. 31% of the media houses that responded said they have paternity leave. This includes Media24, the largest private media house in the sample, led by a woman CEO for almost a decade. A community radio station said all employees have a standard number of "family responsibility days".

But there is still a way to go. A Caxton respondent noted that the company does not make allowances for family responsibility issues that women face, such as suddenly being dropped by a babysitter, while "family responsibilities for men have never seemed like a concern".

It is perhaps linked to the age-old perception that - as a male respondent noted in 2006 - "men are more deserving because they have families to support." Many women also have huge financial commitments like ageing parents to support or children or relatives to educate, yet this is not seen in the context of the traditional view of men as breadwinners.

Finding a balance between work and family[1]

Sexual advances, deciding whether to wear heels or flats, juggling household demands, and finding that inner superwoman - female journalists say that a male-dominated media industry has left them fighting harder.

Gathered at the Women in News Summit at WAN-IFRA's World News Media Congress in Durban in June 2017, female journalists and editors from around the world shared their experiences as leading figures in the media - from having to battle to be considered equal to their male counterparts to juggling family life and being a professional.

Then-chairperson of the South African National Editors Forum (Sanef) Mahlatse Mahlase, who is Eye Witness News (EWN) group editor in chief, said working as a journalist and being female came with many pitfalls.

"You still get people who think women cannot be a boss, or are too young to carry out the job. When female staff members become passionate about a discussion and want to air their opinion, they are called emotional. We really need some super powers to be the mother, wife and journalist always on call and monitoring what's happening in case we miss something that's news. I wish I knew how to be that superwoman."

She said she wished she had set more parameters in her earlier days as a journalist. "I wish I had found the balance earlier. Journalists need family time like any other person, more so to provide that support in dealing with a demanding career. They need their weekends and need to be with their children as well."

---

[1] Leading local and international female journalists describe what happens when they try to strike that balance in this edited report by Arthi Gopi of the Independent on Saturday.

Former editor of *Huffington Post South Africa*, **Verashni Pillay**, said that as a female there was the misconception that "hard work equated to long hours". "In fact, I have seen women who return from maternity leave come to the office with more focus, because they concentrate on the work that needs to be done, so that they can leave the office at a good time to be with their children. In fact, they are more productive," she said.

Helje Solberg, CEO of VGTV in Norway, said she faced a dilemma when returning to work after a year on maternity leave.

"I love being a journalist but I also needed to take care of my baby. They wanted me back in the political department and I told them yes, but on the condition that I could leave at 2pm twice a week. And I got it," she said.

Kjersti LøkenStavrum, CEO of Tinius Trust in Norway, said it was important to have a supportive family when working in the media industry.

"I worked long hours and in fact I was not able to help my children with their homework. Thankfully, they did well, but this is what happens in the industry," she said.

Jordan's **Jumana Ghunaimat**, chief editor at *Al Ghad* paper, said she had to explain to her children that she was "not like the other mums".

"I explained to them that I am different, that their mum travels and does not work at home but in an office. And thankfully, they understood," she said, adding that when she was appointed to her position, the newsroom did not know how to react.

"I was the first editor-in-chief for an Arabic paper. I heard people ask 'how could we deal with her?' It's tough to be a journalist in the Middle East, never mind being a female one," she said.

Conclusions

Women's continued absence from decision-making in the media, especially top decision-making, reflects in the gender wage gap, the difference between the average earnings of women and men in the media. While this chapter could not draw any solid conclusions on trends due to an absence of data, the indications are that if anything this gap is increasing rather than decreasing. A strong recommendation of this report is that all media should routinely calculate and report their gender wage gap, and use this to craft corrective policies.

CHAPTER 4

The Old Boys' Network - Sexism in the Media

Breaking up the Old Boys' Network in the media remains a challenge.

Photo: Gender Links

This research shows it is difficult to "prove" sexism even though to those who experience it - women - it is blatant and painful. So much of sexism relates to cultural practices, institutional culture, sexual harassment that no one else witnessed, jokes, innuendo, the old boys' network where decisions are made, being passed over for promotion, among other intangibles.

Little has changed the overwhelming perception that women are kept back from top positions in newsrooms, and that men who have achieved high office have sewn up that territory for themselves. Most respondents in all three surveys said that ambitious women are denigrated and blocked, or take themselves out of the competition.

Every year that the industry has been surveyed women in the industry have called out the old boys' network. The twist in 2018 is that it is no longer the old white boys' network. In many newsrooms, it had been replaced by a new network - of black men. For women, black or white, however, the effect is the same. In 2018, women are still being blocked by the old boys' clubs.

This soft underbelly of sexism in newsrooms is one of the explanations for why, even as women enter the profession in ever greater numbers, they fail to rise to the top. It explains the powerful subtle forces that hold women back and make them feel uncomfortable in their shoes and in their work space.

This chapter explores what is meant by the old boys' network; what language and attitudes still prevail in newsrooms; how these translate into attitudes and practices that block progress. In the #MeToo/#TotalShutDown era, the chapter also explores the realities of sexual harassment in newsrooms, and what is being done about this. The chapter ends with a case study on sexism and sexual harassment at the SABC.

What is the old boys' network?

The "old boys clubs" work in subtle ways shrouded in patriarchal culture. As one respondent put it: "Women are excluded from the informal discussions which precipitate much of the decisions taken by senior editorial management. This happens in bars, after-work drinking sessions, etc. Despite the fact that women do most of the work in the newsroom, they are overlooked for top positions because the men, who do far less work, have time for self-promotion and networking which facilitates their entry into the top tier."

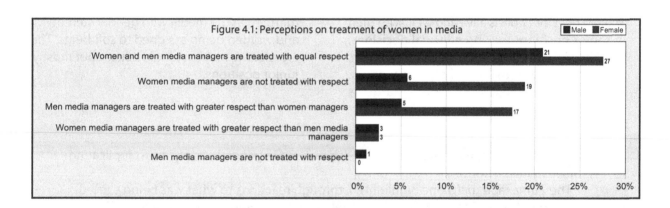

Figure 4.1 shows that the highest proportion of both women (21%) and men (27%) believed that women and men media managers are treated with equal respect. However, 19% of women felt that women media managers are not treated with respect. Seventeen percent of women compared to 5% of men said that men media managers are treated with greater respect compared to women managers. Only 3% of women and men said that women media managers are treated with greater respect than men media managers. Only 1% of men, and no women, thought that male media managers are not treated with respect.

These findings point to the fact that men are perceived as being more respected than women in the media work space, especially by their female co-workers. Perception becomes reality in the eyes of the beholder. This goes a long way in explaining why top leadership positions are still dominated by men, although the ratios are not as pronounced as they were in 2006.

In 2006, it was remarked that "most men - of course there are exceptions - still do not like reporting to or taking instructions from women". In 2018, there are female news editors, female editors and female CEOs, yet attitudes persist. Women's decisions and actions are often questioned while the male counterpart's opinion and actions are more easily accepted. In meetings, the room might go silent while a male colleague is speaking, but a female colleague is interrupted and spoken over. Many women still buy into the belief that women are not capable of leading "because they are emotionally driven" and are "afraid of taking hard decisions".

"Research shows that men are taken more seriously in the corporate world in general, so naturally this will also apply to men in media houses."
"Men are seen as brave individuals who can always come up with good decisions."
"Strong women are often seen as confrontational and troublemakers."
"When we look at South African society and the myriad of capable women and statistics indicating the lack of women in management positions, one can conclude that women are under-represented because of the patriarchal system where men remain preferred candidates for leadership positions."

The old boys' network is alive and well, with men in senior positions making editorial decisions, including in social circles which exclude women, which often blocks the rise of capable women. Patriarchy, as reflected in society at large, is mirrored in the media with gender stereotyping and women being assigned to soft beats. There are more women in media houses but mostly in junior positions.

"The inherent patriarchal structure that's practised in general society is just replicating itself in media houses."
"The Zuma rape trial alone highlighted, through reactions to what was being carried, the complexity of power relationships between men and women. It highlighted the dominant perception of what women are and their place in society."

Sexist attitudes

While there is more awareness of sexist language, jokes, innuendo and sexual harassment in newsrooms, it still exists and is tolerated in 2018, almost as much as it was a decade ago. In 2006 women in the newsroom said they experienced prejudice and being "patronised". Much the same commentary persists in 2018.

"Women are patronised and their opinions do not appear to be taken as seriously as those of men. This can be subtle, like jokes made at their expense when they give their opinions, or teasing. It seems friendly and even affectionate, but it is actually demeaning."

In 2006, men weren't aware that their attitudes towards women in the newsroom were sexist. In 2018, men are more aware - but often their attitudes remain, and they still don't know how and when they are being sexist, which causes frustration.

As an example, here's the 2018 evaluation of a cadet that was accessed: "X is surprisingly reticent for such an attractive young woman". It went a great deal further in 2006: "I regularly see relatively junior women staffers asked (half-jokingly, maybe?) to get tea; referred to as 'girls' and if not exactly sexually harassed, then certainly expected to participate in banter that many might find undermining. Some senior editors still automatically try to date attractive younger female colleagues, but that's thankfully getting rarer."

"I think senior men think they are gender sensitive when in fact they are not. And the fact that they don't know that they don't know is even worse than to argue/debate with those who are outright discriminating."
"There are some men in the work environment who still make sexist remarks disguised as 'jokes' which we often just ignore instead of calling out the person."

In one company, mentioned in all surveys, while sexism is not overt, some comments and behaviour by managers suggest that men are not aware that they are sexist and how that impacts their engagement with women as well as decisions they make about work related matters.

However, another respondent was out of patience with the manifestation of sexist attitude that is still widespread: "Can someone offer a course on why mans-plaining is a bad thing, please? I have a few candidates to suggest."

Dealing with 'subtle' discrimination

Women reporters have to contend with "subtle" discrimination and sidelining in the newsrooms, and also deal with demeaning behaviour, when out in the field, which often results in newsmakers adopting predatory sexual advances towards the reporter.

It can be difficult and hazardous for a female reporter, says **Dianne Hawker**, the head of news at talk radio broadcaster, *Power 98.7*.

While working for the *Sunday Independent*, Hawker was responsible for reporting on judicial and legal matters. Primarily, this involved reporting on court cases and also producing background and investi-gative articles.

She remembers approaching a senior clerk of the court at the South Gauteng High Court and asking for certain documents related to the case. "The official, who was obliged to give me the papers, made a remark that I found totally misplaced. "'Mina ngingumZulu, ukhulume kahle nami'. (I am a Zulu, you must speak properly when speaking to me)."

"The only deduction I could make from that remark was that it was made because I am a woman. It was totally uncalled for," says Hawker. Even the male lawyers would "talk down to you", almost akin to saying "you're a woman, you do not know much about legal matters".

When covering stories in rural areas, female journalists know there is a different set of rules for them compared to those applied to male colleagues. Hawker remembers travelling to Muyexe village in Limpopo to cover water shortages in the area. She travelled with a woman photographer and found that villagers refused to speak to them until the chief gave his approval.

The duo went to the chief's house to seek approval but they were turned away because they were dressed inappropriately, in comfortable jeans, sneakers and t-shirts. They would struggle to tell the story of the village's water crisis if the chief's son had not agreed to speak on his behalf.

It is a reminder that a woman reporter is "less equal" than her male colleague. Hawker considers herself lucky that almost everywhere she has worked, she had women bosses. She disputes the common claim that women bosses are difficult to work with. "I have received tremendous support from the women I've worked with," she says. However, this does not suggest that her long stay in the newsroom has been a bed of roses. "I have had to deal with issues that I thought were inspired by my being a woman," she says.

Hawker says she has encountered "the closing of ranks" by male colleagues, something she refers to as "the boys' club", and which was difficult for a woman to break through. "There were often times when I had to fight to have my stories carried on the front page. The tendency was that only political stories would qualify for front page, and most of the political reporters were male. But I wasn't interested in covering politics - I enjoyed legal reporting. So, I had to stand my ground and fight for the space."

Investigative reporting had its own hazardous offerings and risks. When you are pursuing an investigative story, whoever supplies you with information would want to meet with you in places or in an environment that, for a woman, might not be particularly safe to go to.

"You have to weigh up the risk of going to meet with your informers. You have to assess how much you trust the person you're meeting. If someone wanted to meet me at night, I would make sure that I selected the venue of the meeting and that it was a public place," she says.

Hawker also experienced the "boys' club" when entering management and found that she had to fight for her voice to be heard once again. There was a subtle dismissal of her ideas and she found that she needed to find allies to get her proposals across.

"I had to lobby one of my male colleagues to support me at the diary meetings. I would suggest an idea and it would be shot down. But I knew that I had already briefed him and he agreed that it was a good idea. So when he was asked what he thought of the idea, I knew he would back me up and we would run with my suggested angle. This happened too many times for it to have been a coincidence."

Women still seen as 'soft'

Are women more emotional than men? Should they be relegated to the 'softer' side of journalism, the features and magazines, leaving hard news and investigations to the men? Are they incapable of leadership? Or are they being blocked out of male self-interest?

In 2018, covering stories where violence is involved is still dangerous.

"We often risk our lives while out on stories."
"Women are not encouraged to be in the media industry because of threats and dangers."
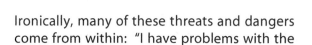

Ironically, many of these threats and dangers come from within: "I have problems with the crew. They are all male and a lot of the time I feel unsafe around them because of intimidation and a lack of respect," said one respondent in broadcasting.

"Women are subjected to backlashing."
"And women outside the newsroom are subjected to threats and victimisation."

Nonetheless, some women are making real inroads into high positions, especially in broadcasting - both commercial and community - and in community newspapers. In most responses from women at community radio stations, they noted that they rose through the ranks, and their work ethic and the fact that their sacrifices were greater than those of the men, was noted. In respect of beats, "hard" beats like politics and economics still tend to go mainly to men, while softer beats like lifestyle and fashion are still predominantly done by women.

Proving yourself with tough beats

Judy Sandison was so outraged by the humiliation dished out by her colleagues that she opted to cover hard news in crime, sport and courts. Sandison, a long serving member of Sanef's Diversity and Ethics Committee, tells her own story:

Early on in my career as the only female reporter in the SABC radio newsroom in Durban I had a couple of experiences that were humiliating but ended up spurring me on to fight back harder.

One evening as I was compiling the hourly news bulletin for Radio Port Natal, a couple of the guys thought it would be amusing to surprise me and wound reams of sticky tape round me to tie me on to my typist chair, spin me round and leave me there.

Another time a chief subeditor came from behind as I was typing up a story, and grabbed both my breasts... hard. When I yelled out, he said: "If you can't take the heat, stay out of the kitchen."

I had started out by being put on lighter beats such as interviewing visiting celebrities, attending mayoral cocktail parties, taking down stock prices and sports scores from stringers, etc.

But these experiences made me so angry that over the next few months I kept pushing to do every tough story, from courts and crime to boxing and rugby, determined to show them I could do anything as a reporter. I gained great field experience!

I was one of the few female reporters in the Parliamentary Press Gallery. Some Cabinet ministers would demand that certain of us attend their news briefings and tell us we had to wear skirts, not trousers.

Three of us were also called "Parlementere Poppies" in a story about us breaking what we now call the glass ceiling and I had some quite pushy passes made at me by an SABC board member at the time and by some MPs at cocktail parties. I was told by a female colleague: you will never get anywhere at the SABC because you are a woman, English-speaking and a feminist!

As the first provincial editor at SABC News, I was also told I "talked too much" in meetings and was too assertive. My first editor told me: over his dead body would there ever be a woman editor. And in 1994 he visited me in my vast office - which had a handy urinal - when I was leading the radio news transformation project nationally as acting editor-in-chief of radio news at Auckland Park in 1994. He lived to see me become what would have been his boss!

Sexual Harassment

As reflected in Figure 4.2, in 2018, 87% of media houses said they had sexual harassment policies, compared to 82% in 2009. Almost all media houses (91%) reported dealing with sexual harassment cases. One company holds workshops on sexual harassment at the workplace - in case potential harassers don't know what's wrong with it.

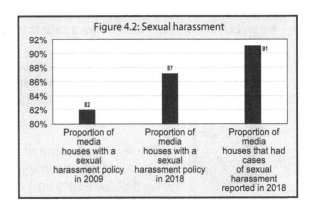

Figure 4.2: Sexual harassment

> "We have found in our internal processes that female staff are harassed. More junior male staff are mostly responsible. Our company policies around this are clear and communicated via email, available on our internal intranet and reinforced at department and staff meetings."

SEXUAL HARASSMENT IS VIOLENCE

A Media24 respondent noted that "under the leadership of our (woman) CEO, incidents of sexual harassment declined rapidly and are now almost unheard of in our business".

Below is an edited version of an article written for *Nasty Women* by Aarti Narsee a former eNCA reporter who is now a Chevenning Scholar at the London School of Economics, MSc Gender, Policy and Inequality. Narsee shares how women journalists experience sexual harassment on a daily basis in South Africa.

None but ourselves - women journalists must speak out!
By Aarti Narsee[1]

"You are so beautiful, are you married?"
"I should have booked you into my hotel room."
"I will rape you."

These are just some of the utterances that I and other women journalists have encountered at some time in our careers. The onlookers who see the work we do daily, whether on TV, radio or in newspaper, often say its "part of the job".

My first question to them would be: "Would you be harassing me or sexualising me If I was a male journalist? The answer is NO. But this happens to us almost every day. My first startling encounter took place when I was a young intern at a print media house. I was keen and eager to build up as many contacts in areas that were of interest to me.

I had made contact with a chief magistrate, who was quite outspoken with the media and useful to me on stories about challenges facing the judiciary. Along with some other journalists, I was invited to attend an annual general meeting. I took this opportunity to introduce myself to him in person, in an effort to continue building a better work relationship for future stories.

That night, after having briefly met him, I received a text message, saying: "Aarti, if I had known you were as beautiful in person as your name, I would have booked a hotel room here for the night."

As I read the message I froze, I was shocked and confused. Was he implying anything sexual here? Experience has taught me that he was. A few years later, the same person asked to meet for coffee, as he was on a trip to Cape Town. I made an excuse to avoid this at all costs. I didn't feel like I would be safe if I met with him.

Then of course there are always personal questions like: "Are you single or married? Can I be your boyfriend?" And let's not forget the politicians who harass us and speak to us differently because we are women.

After speaking to the women journalists, I realised we all shared similar stories. One of my journalist friends is one of the most fearless people I know. She always tends to find herself in the midst of protestors, petrol bombs or tear gas. "I always considered myself to be a brave person...but last year something reminded me of my vulnerability as a female journalist," she says. She recounts that the incident happened while she was covering a protest in Hout Bay and accompanied by her colleague, a male multi-media journalist.

---

[7] Narsee,A. 2018 Women Journalists and Sexual Harassment https://www.nastywomen.org.za/women-journalists-sexual-harassment/

"During the protest things got so intense that at one point I used my phone to file my story. While doing this there were three protesters who told me 'we will rape you if you don't put your phone away'.

"This was a threat they used a few times. They threatened me with the worst kind of sexual violence. It just really brought me back to the reality that I am a woman. They didn't see me as someone doing a job because they didn't say this to my male colleague. They didn't say this to the other male photographers who were also doing their job just like I was," she says.

She adds, "It reminded me that while I might have the ability to do everything that men do, I still need to be so much more aware of my safety, I need to be more vigilant than they need to be. They probably will never have to face the same kind of sexual threat that I would have to."

We are the very same women that cover stories about rape, politics, the burning service delivery issues at protests, tracking legislation at Parliament. We give a voice to those who want to speak out. But who speaks out for us? Who defends us when we are on a story and someone sexualises us or threatens us? No one else, but us!

SABC Commission on Sexism and Sex Harassment

The public broadcaster is committed to diversity but is still struggling with sexual harassment in its newsrooms.   *Photo: Colleen Lowe Morna*

If ever proof were needed that sexual harassment is still a huge issue in newsrooms, it is the establishment of a commission on sexism and sexual harassment by the public broadcaster.

In an interview on the reasons for the establishment of the commission the SABC's Nomsa Philiso says it became "absolutely" necessary to institute an independent commission after "rumours" became louder and louder suggesting sexual misdemeanours were rife at the institution.

Sex abuses at the SABC were not only confined to employees of the public broadcaster but went as far as luring unsuspecting students who would be drawn into sexual acts with miscreant staffers under false pretences.

Philiso was the public broadcaster's acting CEO at the time of the commission's establishment. "There was this unsettling talk about the prevalence of sexual harassment and sexism. We felt the HR department was not the appropriate forum to deal with the matter as it had lost credibility in the eyes of many."

Philiso, who is now group executive for TV, says at about the same time there was talks of editorial interference, and that meant instituting another commission to focus specifically on that aspect.

On the harassment and sexism complaints, Philiso says these mostly affected the freelancers and junior staff. Senior staff and executives were "insulated" against these acts as this level consists mostly of strong women, she says.

The peculiarity of the SABC is that all its production shows - *Generations, Muvhango*; and others - are produced by outside commissioned production houses that are independent of the public broadcaster. These production houses decide who they want on the set and for how long. But not too many people are aware of the arrangement. Most people on the street associate these shows with the SABC, and so they should as they are shown daily on the public broadcaster's screens.

One area - among many - that motivated for the establishment of the commission on sex harassment at the institution is that it was established that there were individuals within the institution who would invite students or young adults into the building under false pretences as producers.

They would tell the unsuspecting students that they would be offered contracts/jobs on one or other productions. And on the back of this promise, demand certain favours, mostly of a sexual nature.

And with regard to permanent employees the target would be those at lower levels of seniority. By virtue of the organisation primarily being a technical operation, especially the television division, junior female staffers would be side-lined from active production work and participation as they would be told that "we will call you when we need your help".

The result would be that junior female employees would feel under-utilised. This practice is more prevalent at the regional offices where supervisory monitoring is virtually non-existent.

Philiso says the process of collecting information from victims has not been as successful as had been initially expected, "because in the case of freelancers, the reluctance to give evidence stemmed from the fear that they would no longer be auditioned for any future productions should they talk about what was happening, and that meant losing their jobs".

Similarly, junior staff at the regions found it difficult to come to give evidence at the commission sitting in Johannesburg "because, for starters, the very culprit who had side-lined you will be the one who must give you permission to travel to head office. So we had to find ways to go to these places (regions), without causing anxiety on the part of those running the regional offices".

"The commission's findings are yet to be tabled to the board, a process that will happen at end of October," says Philiso. However, given what we already know now, and in view of the fact that it is the SABC brand that is on the line, we will insist that as we sign contracts with these independent producers, we make clear that we will have a say in aspects of how they run their operations.

"We want to tighten up on how things are run in order to protect the SABC brand." Philiso says the work of the commission will continue even after it has tabled its recommendations. This is to enable more and more people to come forward and share their experiences. Furthermore, "to ensure that these acts (sexism and sex harassment) are discontinued for ever, we will undertake extensive publicity about what has been shared with us, and in that way, even those who might have had inclinations for such will back off," says Philiso.

Respondents to the perception questionnaire were not as optimistic, however. "The SABC has so many challenges, I don't think gender is a priority at the moment," said one. Another commented: "Gender is not top of our list. Our bigger obstacles are growing our audiences, reaching new audiences, beating our competitors."

Conclusions

Despite the increase in women in senior and top management in the media, sexist attitudes and practices still prevail. These take subtle and not-so-subtle forms, ranging from sexist language and innuendo to more blatant forms of sexual harassment. Women journalists battle these manifestations of patriarchy in the work place and in the field.

One effect is to discourage women from going into "hard" beats where they are most likely to make their mark, and into senior management, where they are not regarded with the same respect as men.

While there is a greater recognition of the issues in 2018 - with more policies and cases of sexual harassment being dealt with, and even a commission being established by the public broadcaster - sexism is still not viewed as a pressing priority. This goes a long way in explaining why, despite the changes in numbers, the underlying realities remain much the same in 2018 as they were in 2006. Senior women who have fought their way through the ranks of the media have a strong message in this chapter to younger women in the media: speak up, speak out!

CHAPTER 5

Cyber misogyny

SADC media women debate online safety at the Forum on Internet Freedom in Africa 2017.   *Photo: Petronella Ngonyama*

Over the past decade of Glass Ceilings research, a new threat to women in the newsroom has emerged: cyber misogyny (hatred of women online), trolling or online social media bullying.

Information and Communication Technologies have been seen as opportunity for women to "catch up" as they had been lagging behind. The struggles that women have faced offline continue to manifest themselves in online spaces which are seen as an opportunity for women to freely express themselves. Added to the physical danger is an electronic one, not imagined in earlier surveys: the prevalence of online trolls. And international surveys and research have confirmed that women are the most targeted group.

Trolling is online bullying and harassment which worldwide studies show affects women more than men. A recent UK study of Twitter abuse targeting celebrities by Demos found that "Journalism is the only category where women received more abuse than men, with female journalists and TV news presenters receiving roughly three times as much abuse as their male counterparts."[1]

The chapter begins with a first-hand account by Ferial Haffajee of trolling and cyberbullying. Haffajee is South Africa's most high profile black woman editor - and is among a few women in the country to have cracked the glass ceiling to become editor of major newspapers. Next it outlines the 2018 survey results on cyber misogyny in South Africa. The chapter then provides the global context and recommendations for addressing cyber misogyny that need to be adapted to our context.

Cyber stalked and trolled
By Ferial Haffajee

 For months, I've looked at them when I'm alone. Quickly, like a dirty secret. The images make me wince with their distortions and insults. I snap my phone shut and move to another screen. Or make a cup of tea. Images are powerful and the designers have very specific messages. That I am a whore, a harridan, an animal and a quisling. I feel shame, and fear that my family will see them and not understand their genesis.

I thought I knew myself better than the crafters of these images do, and so sometimes I've laughed them off when asked about the score of images that have linked me to the hashtag decrying #whitemonopolycapital (white monopoly capital) and which have labelled me variously a presstitute (media prostitute) and a lapdog of the Richemont chairman and South African billionaire Johann Rupert. But upon reflection, the instinct to feel ashamed and to worry about what my less digitally savvy family might think means this kind of trolling works.

Rupert dropped Bell Pottinger as Richemont's public relations specialist, accusing them of running the campaign on white monopoly capital and making him the poster boy. Bell Pottinger was also working for the Gupta family on a hefty retainer. The PR firm is now widely believed to be the masterminds behind efforts to divert attention from the family's capture of the South African state.

Although I have never met Rupert and only spoken to him once or twice, the images had me (or a very badly Photoshopped version) in his lap. There is one of Rupert walking a dog with my face plastered on the pooch and another of him milking a bovine with human visage - mine. The attack is patriarchal and gendered: I am the woman as cow and bitch. The contrivers couldn't get more stereotypical if they tried.

---

[1] Haffajee was editor of the Mail&Guardian and City Press and was editor-at-large on HuffPost South Africa. She is currently associate editor at the Daily Maverick.

Women more prone to cyber bulling than men

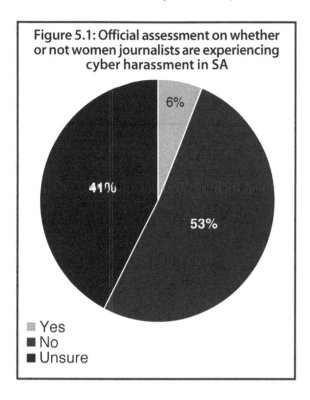

Figure 5.1: Official assessment on whether or not women journalists are experiencing cyber harassment in SA

6%

41%

53%

■ Yes
■ No
■ Unsure

South Africa, it seems, is just waking up to some of these realities. The institutional questionnaire

sent to the HR departments of media houses asked for the first time in 2018 whether women journalists are experiencing cyber harassment. In this official assessment (see Figure 5.2), only 6% said yes; 53% said no and 41% were unsure.

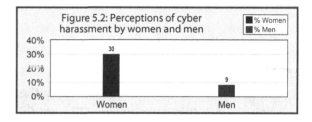

Figure 5.2: Perceptions of cyber harassment by women and men

■ % Women
■ % Men

40%
30%
20%
10%
0%

30

9

Women   Men

The perception questionnaire sent out to five or six employees in each media house tells a different story. As reflected in figure 5.2, 30% women and 9% men agreed that women journalists do face cyber violence. While only a few women reported cyber stalking, quite a few said they had been victims of unknown email or cellphone correspondence issuing violent threats, bullying and trolling, often of a sexual nature.

"When females do stories on certain issues that touch very close to home for certain males, the reaction is a very negative one on social media. Women have drawn a lot of flak on air for challenging the patriarchal perceptions in the past, and still do."

Ways to deal with this new reality were addressed, with respondents calling for media houses to support victims and even locate cyber bullies and stalkers. Suggestions from respondents include hiding the gender of the journalist - possible in print and online - reporting cases to

a senior journalist or to the police, and blocking the perpetrators, if one can identify them. One suggestion is to create a link, an online tracker that will both report such incidents and follow the perpetrators.

Intimidation and cyber bullying

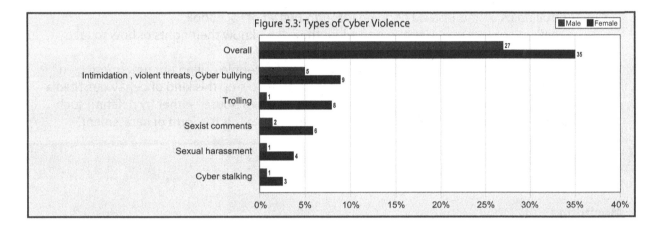

Figure 5.3: Types of Cyber Violence

Describing the types of violence, 9% women and 5% men identified intimidation, violent threats and cyber bullying, while 8% women and 1% men cited trolling. Six percent women and 2% men said they'd experienced sexist comments online; 6% women and 1% men cited sexual harassment, and 3% women and 1% men cited cyber stalking. Twenty one said these incidents were reported, while 57 said they had not. Some respondents said women journalists may be more prone to cyber bullying due to the nature of their work, i.e., that they are reporting on events and issues that may elicit negative male reaction that can and does take to social media.

Internal control

Some respondents felt the media houses should be more interventionist in supporting women journalists in the online space. A suggestion was that legal advice should be freely accessible, and/or workshops held in the newsroom to educate journalists about their rights and how to take action.

"There needs to be some way we can immediately report someone who we see is bullying or trolling us online, instead of going through Twitter or Facebook."
"I think people are easily intimidated when they don't know their rights or how to take action against someone who is threatening."
"Words like *juffroutjie* or *dametjie* are often used by people calling our newsroom or in their online comments on stories. Nothing gets done to stop this kind of behaviour. Media houses should take a stronger stance against this kind of abuse - either by deleting such comments or raising awareness among our readers that this is a form of harassment."

Monitoring

Some respondents suggested appointing a senior member of staff to deal with cyber bullying incidents, or creating a website where such acts can be confidentially reported, backed up by IT software that can track and identify perpetrators.

One respondent reported that News 24 had in one instance switched off the "comments" function, due to sexist and racist comments that were made.

"Have someone senior - a woman - tasked with receiving and sensitively handling complaints or comments that are made to her in confidence (through a "hotline" that can be anonymous too)."
"Appoint a dedicated staff member to monitor all the incidents and report back to management, so swift action can be taken against the perpetrator."
"Create a link to report such incidents and also an online tracker that will follow the perpetrators."
"The IT department should build strong defensive software that will protect all employees."
"A list of perpetrators and their details must be kept, so that they can be blocked from all our social media pages and blacklisted from any future interactions."

No intervention?

Other respondents felt that cyber bullying is "part of the job", and that management and/or the police should only get involved if the threats became serious.

> "It kind of goes with the job. I do think if it becomes something serious like sexual harassment management needs to assist and guide the journalist through professional procedures."
> "We can only notify the responsible authorities. We have little policing powers to control cyber activities of the public."
> "One cannot hold perpetrators accountable in an online environment, as it is totally ungoverned. If the trolling happens on our own sites, we block and remove commentators."
> "We should be aware of the importance of using security features on cellphones, and be conscious of activity on social media platforms that can attract unwelcome responses."

Cyber misogyny - the global picture

While the South African situation does not look so bad, minus a few high-profile cases such as Haffajee, abroad it is rampant.

One study shows female journalists face "rampant" online harassment. The following is an extract from a piece by Denise-Marie Ordway in the Journalist's Resource, based at Harvard's Shorenstein Centre on Media, Politics and Public Policy.

In-depth interviews with dozens of female journalists from across the globe reveal that women in news face various forms of online harassment, from sexist remarks and inappropriate requests to threats of rape, a study published in the international, peer-reviewed journal Journalism finds.

Researchers also learned that the strategies women use to deal with such abuse can disrupt their newsroom routines, even prompting some to change the way they report the news. They described the harassment as "rampant."

Akua Gyekye and Caroline Millin, Facebook public policy team talking about online safety tools at Facebook, Johannesburg.   *Photo: Petronella Ngonyama*

"Consistently, the journalists we interviewed saw online gendered harassment as hampering their efforts to report the news, engage with the communities they cover, or have a voice in the digital sphere," writes the research team, led by Gina Masullo Chen, an assistant professor of journalism at the University of Texas at Austin.

The study contains vivid descriptions of the abuses women said they faced, described in their own words. Some examples:

An online editor from Germany: "The feedback [on this article] was not criticism, it was threats, it was death threats, it was calls for rape."

A veteran newspaper journalist in the US, on receiving hundreds of messages after writing about Donald Trump from the perspective of a Muslim woman: "I was shocked by the dehumanization and demonization that exploded on Twitter and Facebook as well as direct email to the point to where I thought I should get security cameras."

A broadcast journalist in the US, on people leaving misogynistic comments on her professional Facebook page so often that she blocks certain words: "I have moderation on my page for the words 'sexy', 'hot' or 'boobs'."

A video producer in the United Kingdom: "Now and then I'll get comments thrown at me, purely just about my hair colour. I will get comments about being [a] blonde and not being intelligent enough because of my hair."

Reporters are often encouraged, and sometimes required, to promote their work and interact with audiences online. But audience engagement can have ugly consequences as some people use Twitter, Facebook and other online platforms to attack members of the press. Of the 75 female journalists interviewed for the study, 73 said they had experienced gendered harassment online, or harassment that focuses specifically on their gender or sexuality. TV journalists reported experiencing harassment most often.

The journalists interviewed work or have worked in the United States, Germany, India, Taiwan and the United Kingdom. Chen and her colleagues sought out women of different ages, races and experience levels, representing a variety of media outlets and newsroom types. While the small sample of 75 people isn't representative of female journalists as a whole, the researchers write that their goal was to "find meaning through the female journalists' words, not make generalisable inferences."

"The main takeaway for journalists and news organisations is that harassment of female journalists is a serious problem that needs to be addressed," Chen told Journalist's Resource, based at Harvard's Shorenstein Centre on Media, Politics and Public Policy. The example that follows from the Philippines makes a powerful case from the global south on why this is so:

Lessons from the Philippines on cyber misogyny
By Julie Posetti

Maria Ressa is a former CNN war correspondent, but none of her experiences in the field prepared her for the destructive campaign of gendered online harassment that has been directed at her since the election of President Rodrigo Duterte in 2016.

"I've been called ugly, a dog, a snake, threatened with rape and murder," says Ressa. How many times has she received online death threats? She's lost count. "Gosh, there have been so many!"

In addition to being threatened with rape and murder, she's been the subject of hashtag campaigns like #ArrestMariaRessa and #BringHerToTheSenate, designed to whip online mobs into attack mode, discredit both Ressa and her online news site Rappler and chill her reporting.

Every journalist in the country reporting independently on the Duterte presidency is subjected to rampant and highly coordinated online abuse, she says, especially if they're female. "It began a spiral of silence. Anyone who was critical or asked questions about extrajudicial killings was attacked, brutally attacked. The women got it worst." "The system is set up to silence dissent - designed to make journalists docile. We're not supposed to be asking hard questions, and we're certainly not supposed to be critical." She admits that the constant attacks do make her think twice about doing stories that will be lightning rods for attacks. "But then I go and do the story even harder! I just refuse to let intimidation win."

Her response to the threats includes investigative reporting on the intertwined problems of online harassment, disinformation and misinformation. She believes in "throwing sunlight" on the abusers.

But after *Rappler* published a feature series mapping the corrosive impacts of organised political trolling on the Philippines in October 2016, the onslaught of abuse and threats of violence escalated dramatically. The series deployed big data analysis techniques to establish that a "sock puppet network" of 26 fake Facebook accounts was influencing nearly three million other Philippines-based accounts. Behind the "sock puppets" were three "super trolls", as Ressa describes them.

Their aim was to publish misinformation and foment targeted attacks. "They would plant messages within groups, inflaming the groups who would then become a mob to attack the target," she says.

In the days following publication of the *Rappler* series titled *Propaganda War: Weaponising the Internet*, she received on average 90 hate messages an hour. Among these was what she describes as the first credible death threat against her. The messages continued for months. "It happened so fast and at such frequency, I didn't realise how unnatural it was," she says.

In early 2017, Ressa received another threat that stunned her. It was the kind of threat that women journalists are increasingly familiar with internationally: a call for her to be gang-raped and murdered. A young man wrote on *Rappler*'s Facebook page: *"I want Maria Ressa to be raped repeatedly to death, I would be so happy if that happens when martial law is declared, it would bring joy to my heart."*

Ressa responded like a digital journalist who understands the power of audiences. She asked her online communities to assist in identifying the threat-maker, who was using a Facebook account in a fake name. They came through. With her supporters' help, Ressa was able to identify the man as a 22-year-old university student. When his university learned of his activities, he was forced to call Ressa and apologise.

Then, in the middle of an online storm triggered by a deliberately misleading report on a fake news site that misquoted Ressa, active and former members of the Philippines military piled on with abuse and threats. Again, she activated her own online communities in response, and one "netizen" wrote an open letter to the chief of the armed forces of the Philippines, General Eduardo Ano, asking him to intervene.

This activation of her networks worked. General Ano was upset by the incident, ordered an investigation and issued an official apology: "We publicly apologise to Miss Maria Ressa for the emotional pain, anxiety and humiliation those irresponsible comments and unkind remarks might have caused her," he wrote.

Ressa decided to upgrade security in *Rappler*'s newsrooms and provide protection for the journalists facing the worst of the online attacks, adding that: "It's crossed the line where I do worry about safety. When you have people getting killed every night in the drug war and you have these online threats, you have no choice as a responsible corporation but to increase security for the people who work for you."

And she's keeping her legal options open. The sheer number of attacks means that it's not possible to follow through on each one, Ressa says. But Rappler is recording every online threat and storing the data for possible future legal action. She acknowledges the enormity of the challenge confronting Facebook, but Ressa is adamant that the only way forward is for the social media giant to take responsibility for the problem and accept its role as a news publisher.

(This is an edited extract from "An Attack on One Is an Attack on All: Successful initiatives to protect journalists and combat impunity", published by UNESCO and launched at a United Nations conference in Geneva in June 2017).

First steps against cyber misogyny

While highlighting the potential of social media channels to act as conduits for women's empowerment and solidarity, experts acknowledge the growing impact of "cyber misogyny" on women journalists.

In an article titled *"Trends in Newsrooms: Business of Gender Equality"* in *The Media Online*, Posetti (2015) said that important steps are being undertaken globally to provide training for women journalists to fight cyber misogyny.

Australian journalist, journalism educator and feminist activist Jenna Price, quoted in the Posetti article, says the Australian Broadcasting Corporation (ABC) has begun "social media defence" classes as an intervention, a strategy she welcomed, saying media employers"… need to practice responsible corporate citizenship and ensure their staff have the social media skills AND the emotional support required… it needs policy, strategy and action."

Making the Internet safe for the next generation of women journalists.   *Photo: Colleen Lowe Morna*

However, if newsrooms themselves remain bastions of male domination, harassment and sexism, better management of the effects of cyber misogyny will not have a major impact on new moves to target women's empowerment in, and through, the media.

Recommendations globally for managing cyber misogyny

1. Acknowledge the problem and take the impacts seriously.
2. Provide specific training for women journalists to help them deal with cyber-misogyny.
3. Stimulate senior management awareness of the issues.
4. Invest in community engagement manage-ment (including clear policies and guidelines for intervention, along with effective abuse reporting tools).
5. Devote editorial resources to coverage of these issues.
6. Consider adding misogyny to comment moderation guideline definitions.
7. Dedicate more staff to understanding and performing moderation.
8. Employ more senior women moderators/community managers.
9. Advocate the uptake of abuse reporting tools like the Women Action Media initiative by social media companies.

Conclusions

Cyber misogyny may well be an emerging phenomenon in South Africa, but like the speed of the social media that spawned it, is guaranteed to spiral out of control if not addressed seriously. This is why a whole chapter has been dedicated to this issue in the 2018 Glass Ceiling report. Ferial Haffajee's powerful testimony should be a wake-up call to media decision-makers to heed the recommendations emerging globally for addressing this ill, lest it undermines all the other gains being made.

The immediate remedies need to be placed in the broader context of the systemic changes needed. Cyber misogyny is both a cause and consequence of the sexist stereotypes that pervade our media houses. The surest long-term solutions are to rid not only our newsrooms, but our entire societies, of the misogyny that finds its way to, and mutates on social media platforms. Systemic and holistic solutions are needed.

CHAPTER 6

Conclusions and Recommendations

GL Media Manager Tarisai Nyamweda (foreground) reviewing research questionnaires.   *Photo: Gender Links*

With each successive *Glass Ceilings* research study, the issues have become less about numbers, and more about the underlying patriarchal culture of the media that makes it inhospitable to women, despite rhetoric to the contrary.

The 2018 study finds that there have been dramatic shifts in the race and gender composition of media houses since 2006. Black men are now well represented in senior and top ranks of the media relative to their strengths in the population. The proportion of white men, while still higher than their strength in the population and almost double that of white women in media decision-making, has concurrently declined over this period.

At 40% in senior management and 30% in top management, black women - who comprise 46%

of the population - are still least well represented in media decision-making. However, their numbers have increased dramatically since 2006 when black women comprised a mere 6% of top media decision makers.

Here is a comment from 2006, which was repeated almost verbatim in 2018: "The newsroom culture is still masculine and the men's club or 'old boys' network', from which women are excluded, still rules. For example, the male editor invites only men to eat with him in the canteen at lunchtime - and, unbeknown to him, all the women in the newsroom talk about this."

Why, under the circumstances, is there still such a large gender pay gap? And why is sexism still so rife in the media? A key theme that emerges in the study is that in 2018 gender is regarded as much less of a factor compared to race and the financial pressures that the media faces. *Glass Ceilings 2018* also shows signs of both a feminist backlash, and an increased anger and assertiveness by women in the media against sexism, which may be the result of the general *zeitgeist* of the times globally and nationally.

Race and financial concerns take precedence over gender

In 2018, respondents generally agreed that issues of gender are secondary to race. The instant response to race transgressions within the corporate setting, whilst important, is never matched by a similar response to gender - be that the gender pay gap, sexual harassment, or career advancement.

 "Race is front and centre of every discourse in South Africa at the moment."
"Race is still the most important issue we need to deal with, both as an industry and as a country. "
"Racism is tackled first because it affects men."

This causes frustration, as few women of colour are represented in top positions, even in 2018. Yet there are plenty of female candidates for these positions. "If I look at my own newspaper, as well as the graduating class for my journalism diploma, there were more women than men in both. However in my newspaper the top leadership positions are heavily skewed towards men," said one respondent.

Harsh economic realities are also pushing the gender question aside in 2018. With pressure to survive in the digital age, and cutbacks and restructuring a common occurrence, the focus is primarily on economic survival, exploring other revenue streams and cutting costs where possible.

Feminist backlash

The feminist backlash, i.e. resistance to transformation in media houses due to heightened pressure, is possibly the reason for the decreased numbers of women in top positions in the newsroom. Women editors, for example, have decreased, even though it must be acknowledged that there are two women who are at the top of two of the biggest television companies in the country: the SABC's group executive for news and current affairs Phathiswa Magopeni, since March 2018, and eNCA editor in chief Mapi Mahlangu, since 2017.

The feminist backlash is evidenced in the abuse that women suffer online in cyber bullying and trolling incidents. Sexist jokes, the patriarchal culture and the boys' network remains. Progress can be seen in the boldness of the comments, where women speak out against sexism and call out the gender pay gap. Still, some things have not changed at all: with the old boys' network and a patriarchal culture still a reality, women are overlooked for promotions and most staff in the newsrooms, whether they are men or women, do not know if affirmative gender policies exist.

Even though women in the newsroom are less militant in their assertiveness compared to their broader society, they could be finally taking their lead from here to say #TimesUp. A speaking out culture appears to be emerging.

Both academic and civil society research have come up with some possible recommendations that could help influence the way media institutions prioritise gender equality in media. This study also seeks to come up with recommendations that can help inform the media sector in its quest for transformation in line with women's empowerment.

Studies also referred to in this report have made recommendations and suggested actions which could be taken to address the long-standing problems, both structural and cultural, which impede women's efforts to pursue their career aspirations and fulfil their potential. It really does not make sense at any level, ethical or business-wise, to deliberately to underutilise the talents of 50% of the media workforce, and one significant problem in working for change has been a lack of knowledge by media managers about the scale of the issue and potential solutions. It is within this context that the recommendations are stronger than in any previous *Glass Ceilings* research.

Recommendations

In search of answers: Portia Kobue, currently the news editor at Kaya FM.
Photo: Colleen Lowe Morna

Ownership and control: Tapping into Marxist theories on capitalism, those who own the means of production have the power to influence the means of socialisation as well as the production of knowledge. In this case, ownership and control of the media sector are critical areas where women can begin to influence the organisational behaviours, attitudes and practices and even the content that is produced. Ownership of media by gender sensitive and aware women and men will set the media on a path of better gender responsive behavior in the media sector.

Gender and diversity policies: All media houses and newsrooms need a diversity policy that includes gender. Knowledge of equity laws and gender policies should be spread through workplace training and awareness. This includes race, class, and sexual orientation, religion and cultures, gender fluidity and transgenderism.

Setting targets: Media houses need to come up with their own quotas that can help to deliberately increase participation of women in the media. This is not to say ill trained women or unqualified women should be given positions. Edit bias out of your hiring and selection processes.

The human brain is designed to use bias to navigate complex reality. It is not, however, designed to create equitable hiring and panellist selection procedures. Media houses should also put in place mechanisms for checks and balances with respect to gender equality targeting to reach at least 50% representation at all levels by 2030. These targets must be accompanied by action plans that set a more structured path for reaching these targets.

Ban sexism: All discriminatory practices must be removed from media companies and newsrooms. All sexist language in reporting, or in discourse between reporters, editors and managers, should be banned - with sanctions imposed where there are transgressions. There should be a policy in place to ban sexism, based on an investigation into what the institutional practices are, what the structural inequalities are, and the cultural norms and values in different newsrooms that contribute to the discrimination against women. Call out sexism at every opportunity, say #Timesup. Name, shame and shun sexists, sexist behaviour and sexual harassment. Every single time there is a "manel" or male only panel at a media or journalism conference, call this out.

Call out "mansplaining" (men explaining to women things they are well aware of) and mind conversation culture. According to award-winning Australian journalist Julie Posetti and former CNN war correspondent Maria Ressa, male dominance on panels and in meetings, interruption of women who are speaking, or "mansplaining" are common ways that women's voices are silenced in work environments.[1]

Let women pull back, and lean in when ready. Just because a woman refuses promotion when she wants to focus more on her family doesn't mean she will never want to put her career in high gear again. Many women choose to focus on their children when they are young. Once children reach a certain level of independence, their parents' capacity to "lean in" tends to rebound strongly.[2]

Open spaces for women to speak out: Women in 2006, 2008 and 2018 consistently say they feel patronised and demeaned. Thus there should be sessions in newsrooms where their voices can be heard and they can explain how and why they feel this way. Workshops or seminars coming out of this research should be held to enhance the understanding of patriarchy, a term everyone uses today but is not necessarily understood by everyone in the media.

Transparency, especially on wages! One of the concrete ways to understand the impact of patriarchy is to agitate for all companies to reveal their gender pay gap, following the example of the BBC, and then insist that there is a timeframe to rectify this.

Employment conditions must change to include parenthood time: Men need to take equal responsibility for children so that women are not discriminated against. There is a need for professional bodies following the death of the South African Union of Journalists (SAUJ) and the weakening of Media Workers Association of South Africa (MWASA). This means that women can't go anywhere with their sexism stories.

Gender equality initiatives must be mainstreamed: We need to stop treating the gender equality conversation as peripheral, according to UNISA communications lecturer Julie Reid, speaking at a UNESCO panel on World Press Freedom Day (2018) in Ghana, when she also urged that we recognise that this is potentially the most

---

[1] See their 14 principles of gender equality in the news industry, which all countries can use. (https://www.icfj.org/news/how-end-misogyny-news-industry-open-letter-international-journalism-community).
[2] Ibid

important issue with regard to the entire media ecology.

Self-monitoring: Media houses need to conduct annual audits of numbers of women in the newsroom, as editors, in management, on boards, as owners of media, and voices of women in the media/reportage itself. These should be used to constantly adjust plans and targets until gender equality is achieved in and through the media.

Endnote: A framework for putting gender on the media agenda

 Mary Papayya is a founding Sanef member on both radio and print platforms. She is an activist on gender issues and has often been called upon to deliver papers to seminars and conferences on the subject. She is a founding Sanef editor. Below is the framework that she uses and follows when delivering her papers:

To succeed in achieving gender parity, journalists are encouraged to follow a gender-sensitive framework. From a business perspective, senior management is empowered to understand that gender and women issues are critical to the bottom line. Women make up more than half of the country's population and are economically active citizens and key decision makers.

Journalists have to understand the role media plays in presenting stories that project diverse voices - both men and women. For gender to be on the news agenda, the following are critical:
1. Commitment by the news leadership to promote gender-sensitive stories and non-discriminatory reporting as a rule.
2. Top management support to provide an enabling environment for gender-sensitive reporting and storytelling, including budgets for training and internal support for encouraging a gender-sensitive and equity-driven organisation.
3. Training of all journalists - men and women - on gender and gender-sensitive reporting and gender-neutral language and non-stereotyping.
4. Mainstreaming of gender stories and equitable reporting on gender as part of the daily news diary.
5. The hiring of women journalists also assists in the mainstreaming of the gender objective in the newsroom.

"In some instances, notwithstanding the deadline and bottom-line pressures," she says, "the newsroom has to have gender champions - men and women - who are tasked with promoting stories with women's voices. Stories on issues affecting women are also a priority. Contact databases in the newsroom must be updated to include women newsmakers, women spokespersons and women experts. Women reporters in newsrooms are encouraged to pursue the non-traditional beats like sports, politics, crime and business.

"From a community perspective, we drive the agenda through making the voices of women in all communities heard. In instances where we encounter challenges with women not speaking out due to cultural and traditional practices, we highlight the issues as a news story through the use of expert analysis and commentary. Increasingly this kind of reportage also educates women and communities and encourages them to speak to our journalists."

Papayya says she is convinced that the input made in advancing gender sensitivity and equity in the news narrative is still applicable. "It is clear that the issue of gender-sensitive reporting still remains a big challenge in our newsrooms in 2018. The portrayal of women's voices on radio, television, in print and online needs redress."

Given the shrinking of major news operations, downsizing of staff numbers and the demands made on journalists, the issue has taken a back seat. It needs revival and resurrection by leaders at all levels of our newsrooms - radio, television, print and online.

"But it's not all doom and gloom," she says. "There are success areas. These can be achieved through programmes and segments dedicated to women in all sectors of the media and in society, economically, politically and socially. We need to encourage these narratives and conversations. They must be highlighted at critical platforms and must be celebrated."

Journalists@Work - SA International Women's Day.

Photo courtesy Trevor Davies

Gender Links Gender in the Media Policy Checklist

Affirmative Action Policy
✓ Do you have an affirmative action policy?
✓ Does law prescribe the affirmative action policy or is it your own?
✓ Does it spell out precise quotas or targets for male and female representation?
✓ Are these broken down by rank?
✓ Are there timeframes for achieving this?
✓ Is there a plan and resources allocated for achieving this (for example, additional empowerment strategies for women, if required?)?
✓ Do you keep regular staff records, disaggregated by gender?
✓ Does management regularly monitor and evaluate these?

Recruitment
✓ Do you advertise using a variety of communication channels, including direct interaction, that ensure men and women are equally reached?
✓ Do you actively encourage women to apply?
✓ Is there anything in the way your advertisements are phrased that could discourage women from applying?
✓ Do you have initiatives to encourage young women to take up careers in the media?

Selection
✓ Are your selection panels gender balanced?
✓ Do you ensure a minimum quota for women in the short-listing process?
✓ Do the same standards apply to women and men in the interview process? For example, would you ask a man whether he was married and had children?
✓ How are family considerations raised and addressed in the interview process?

Work environment
✓ Do you have any initiatives in place that promote a gender friendly work environment?
✓ If someone told a sexist joke at your workplace how would others respond? Would there be any sanction?
✓ Do you have a sexual harassment policy?
✓ Do you offer flexi- hours?
✓ Have you taken advantage of IT to you allow work from home under certain conditions?
✓ Do you ensure the safety of all your employees, for example with regard to their transportation to and from work, especially from certain locations and at certain hours?

Family friendly practices
✓ Do you have a maternity policy in place? What are its provisions?
✓ Are there stereotypes in your newsroom concerning the ability of women to perform their journalistic tasks, for example presenting programmes on television while they are pregnant? What have you done to correct these?
✓ Do you ensure that the careers of women journalists are not adversely affected by maternity breaks?
✓ Do you offer paternity leave?

✓ Do you have a policy on breast- feeding?
✓ Do you have child- care facilities?

On the job experience
✓ Is there a gender balance on all your beats?
✓ Are women encouraged to go into non- traditional areas of reporting?
✓ Are women encouraged and supported to take up technical sides of the job, for example as camerawomen in television or photojournalists in the print media?
✓ To the extent that there are physical constraints, for example, the weight of a camera, how have you used advances in technology to overcome this constraint to women's entry into this sphere of work?
✓ To the extent that women may be more exposed to danger than men because of their sex (for example to the danger of rape or sexual harassment) while on the job, what measures have you taken to ensure their security? Have you consciously avoided the easy way out- to simply exclude them from that beat?

Capacity building
✓ Do all your employees have access to staff development programmes, and are these offered at suitable hours?
✓ Do you target women for training?
✓ Do you have mentorship programmes in place?
✓ Are these specifically targeted at women?
✓ Does the organisation offer assertiveness training and are men and women equally encouraged to undergo this training?

Promotion
✓ Do you have a clearly defined and transparent promotion policy?
✓ Do you have a minimum quota for women at all levels of the organisation?
✓ Do you have any measures in place to assist women to achieve these positions on merit?
✓ Do you have a roster of potential women candidates for top posts?
✓ When you head hunt, do you specify gender as one of the criteria to be considered in sourcing suitable candidates?

GENDER MANAGEMENT SYSTEM

Champions
✓ Is there a champion for the gender policy in your organisation?
✓ Is this person at management level?

Governance level
✓ To what extent does the board/management regard gender mainstreaming as a priority?

Administrative level
✓ To what extent does the management of the organisation take gender mainstreaming seriously?
✓ To what extent does all staff take gender mainstreaming as their responsibility?
✓ Are gender considerations built into the overall performance management system?
✓ To what extent is performance in this area measured and rewarded?
✓ To what extent do turnover and lack of continuity and "institutional memory" hinder gender mainstreaming in the organisation?
✓ Are gender resource materials available and accessible?

Structures

Formal
✓ What specific structures have been created for gender mainstreaming?
✓ Do these include the human resource, editorial and advertising departments?
✓ Is there a committee that includes all three?
✓ Is there a gender structure/unit/focal point?
✓ At what level is the gender focal point employed?
✓ What access to/ influence on decision makers, does the gender focal point have?
✓ What other responsibilities does the gender focal point have?
✓ Has the GFP received gender training?
✓ Does the GFP have clear terms of reference?
✓ Is gender part of the GFP job description or is it an- add on?

Informal
✓ What informal structures have been created to encourage understanding and buy in? (For example a gender forum, brown bag lunches)?
✓ Do they include men and women?
✓ Are women encouraged to form support networks and structures?
✓ Are these structures accorded respect and status and given time to meet?
✓ Do these structures network with civil society?

Analytical Capacity
✓ Has the whole organisation undergone gender training?
✓ What form did this take?
✓ Has there been further gender training linked to various areas of responsibility within the organisation?
✓ Did the training have the support of management?
✓ How has gender training been perceived in the organisation?
✓ What has been the tangible impact of gender training?

Monitoring, evaluation and resource allocation
✓ Do you have an internal system to undertake content analysis?
✓ Is gender one of the criteria?
✓ What gender indicators have been developed?
✓ Are statistics disaggregated by gender?
✓ Does content analysis examine: a) events and issues through the voices of both men and women b) stories highlighting the impact of events on men and women? c) Thematic analysis to ensure that issues covered reflect gender challenges?
✓ Do you engage with research findings by civil society, private sector and other bodies on the way in which gender is covered by the media, and on sexist attitudes in society?
✓ Are there internal mechanisms for monitoring the overall gender policy including conditions of service and how they impact on men and women?
✓ How is the budget divided up within each programme?
✓ What is the effect of this with regard to advancing gender equality?
✓ How do women benefit from the budget compared to men?
✓ Would the budget need to shift to address gender objectives more effectively?
✓ Is there an annual review of the implementation of the gender policy?

References

1. ANC. (2013). The Battle for Ideas. ANC (2013) Communications and the Battle for Ideas: 53rd National Conference. Mangaung, December 2012. http://www.anc.org.za/docs/res/2013/resolutions53r.pdf

2. Committee to Protect Journalists (2018). Record number of journalists' jailed as Turkey, China and Egypt pay scant price for repression. https://cpj.org/reports/2017/12/journalists-prison-jail-record-number-turkey-china-egypt.php. Accessed: 2 February, 2018.

3. Chen, Gina Masullo etc. (2018). You really have to have a thick skin: A cross-cultural perspective on how online harassment influences female journalists. Journalism. http://journals.sagepub.com/stoken/default+domain/10.1177/1464884918768500/full. Editor's note: Chen created a white paper to explain the study's findings, written for a general audience. You can find it on the University of Texas at Austin's Center for Media Engagement website.

4. Daniels, G. (2012). Fight for Democracy: The ANC and the Media in South Africa. Johannesburg. Wits Press.

5. Daniels, G (2013). State of the Newsroom, South Africa, 2013. Transitions and Disruptions. Johannesburg. Wits Journalism.

6. Daniels, G. (2014). State of the Newsroom, South Africa, 2014: Disruptions Accelerated. Johannesburg. Wits Journalism.

7. Freedom of Expression Institute (FXI) (2008). The Media and the Law: a Handbook for Community Journalists. Johannesburg. Freedom of Expression Institute (FXI).

8. Gender Links 2017. SADC Gender Protocol Barometer .

9. Guibourg, Clara (2017). BBC facing backlash from female stars after gender pay gap revealed. BBC News. https://www.bbc.com/news/business-43668187)

10. Mahlatse, M. (2017). Sanef statement on the treatment of journalists. The 54th ANC elective conference.

11. Gumani, Tuwani (2018). Email Interview. 12 July 2018.

12. Nevill, G (2018). Journalist bloodbath: new beat research to find out what happens to journos and journalism. The Media Online. http://themediaonline.co.za/2018/07/journalist-bloodbath-new-beat-research-to-find-out-what-happens-to-journos-and-journalism/ Accessed 30 August 2018.

13. Ho, K (2018). Women and minorities are paid the least in newsrooms: report. Columbia Journalism Review. https://www.cjr.org/business_of_news/women-minorities-salary-newsrooms.php

14. Ndlovu, S and Nyamweda, T. 2015. Whose News Whose Views. SADC Gender and Media Progress Study. Gender Links. Johannesburg.

15. Reid, J (2018). More than 300 journalists join Globe effort on freedom of press editorials. Boston Globe. https://www.bostonglobe.com/metro/2018/08/14/newspapers-join-globe-effort-freedom-press-editorials/yvvZ0yepu8j1lJ3G3qYbSJ/story.html

16. Ordway, Denise-Marie (2018). Study shows female journalists face 'rampant' online harassment. Journalist's Resource at Harvard Kennedy School Shorenstein Center. https://journalistsresource.org/studies/society/news-media/female-journalists-harassment-online-research. Accessed 29 August, 2018

17. Haffajee, F (2017). The Gupta Fake News factory and me. HuffPost SA. https://www.huffingtonpost.co.za/2017/06/05/ferial-haffajee-the-gupta-fake-news-factory-and-me_a_22126282/

18. Posetti, J (2015). Trends in Newsrooms: Business of Gender Equality. The Media Online. http://themediaonline.co.za/2015/08/trends-in-newsrooms-business-of-gender-equality/

19. Ordway, Denise-Marie (2018). Study shows female journalists face 'rampant' online harassment. Journalist's Resource at Harvard Kennedy School Shorenstein Center. https://journalistsresource.org/studies/society/news-media/female-journalists-harassment-online-research. Accessed 29 August, 2018.

20. Haffajee, F (2017). The Gupta Fake News factory and me. HuffPost SA. https://www.huffingtonpost.co.za/2017/06/05/ferial-haffajee-the-gupta-fake-news-factory-and-me_a_22126282/

21. Schmidt, C. (2018). Digging for Dung, unearthing corruption. Nieman Journalism Lab at Harvard. https://www.google.com/url?rct=j&sa=t&url=http://www.niemanlab.org/2018/01/digging-for-dung-unearthing-corruption-this-south-african-investigative-nonprofit-could-help-take-down-the-president/ accessed 2 February, 2018.

22. TimesLive (2017). SARS takes Jacques Pauw to court https://www.timeslive.co.za/news/south-africa/2017-12-19-sars-takes-jacques-pauw-to-court/ accessed 2 Feb, 2018.

23. Vale, Louise (2018). Email Interview. May 2018.

24. Rodny-Gumede, Y (2015). Women's voices missing in public discourse. The Journalist.

25. Waterson, Jim (2018). BBC reduces gender pay gap to 8.4%. The Guardian. https://www.theguardian.com/media/2018/jul/04/bbc-reduces-gender-pay-gap

SADC PROTOCOL ON GENDER AND DEVELOPMENT

ARTICLE 29: GENDER IN MEDIA, INFORMATION AND COMMUNICATION

Enact legislation, and develop national policies and strategies including professional guidelines and codes of conduct to prevent and address gender stereotypes and discrimination in the media.

Ensure gender is mainstreamed in all information, communication and media policies, programmes, laws and training in accordance with the Protocol on Culture, Information and Sport and other regional and international commitments by Member States on issues relating to media, information and communication.

Encourage the media and media-related bodies to mainstream gender in their codes of conduct, policies and procedures, and adopt and implement gender aware ethical principles, codes of practice and policies in accordance with the Protocol on Culture, Information and Sport.

Take measures to promote the equal representation of men and women in the ownership of, and decision making structures of the media.

Take measures to discourage the media from:

- Promoting pornography and violence against all persons, especially women and children;

- Depicting women as helpless victims of violence and abuse;

- Degrading or exploiting women, especially in the area of entertainment and advertising, and undermining their role and position in society; and

- Reinforcing gender oppression and stereotypes.

Encourage the media to give equal voice to women and men in all areas of coverage, including increasing the number of programmes for, by and about women on gender specific topics and that challenge gender stereotypes.

Take appropriate measures to encourage the media to play a constructive role in the eradication of gender based violence by adopting guidelines which ensure gender sensitive coverage.

ARTICLE 30: UNIVERSAL ACCESS TO INFORMATION, COMMUNICATION AND TECHNOLOGY

Put in place information and communication technology policies and laws in the social, economic and political development arena for women's employment, regardless of race, age, religion, or class. These policies and laws shall include specific targets developed through an open and participatory process in order to ensure women's and girl's acess to information and communication technology.

Printed in the United States
By Bookmasters